Previous Titles by Rodney Boyd

Chewing the Daily Cud, Volume 1
Chewing the Daily Cud, Volume 2
Chewing the Daily Cud, Volume 3
Speaking & Hearing the Word of God
Pro-Verb Ponderings
Never Run A Dead Kata

CHEWING THE DAILY CUD

Volume 4

Jarin,

Keep chewing on the Word of God

Psalm 27:13

Rodney

CHEWING THE DAILY CUD
Volume 4

92 Daily Ruminations on the Word of God

by

RODNEY BOYD

WordCrafts

Chewing the Daily Cud, Volume 4
91 Daily Ruminations on the Word of God
Copyright © 2017
Rodney Boyd

Cover design and author photo by David Warren

All rights reserved. No part of this book may be reproduced, stored in a retrieval system, or transmitted in any form or by any means – electronic, mechanical, photocopy, recording, or otherwise – without the prior written permission of the publisher. The only exception is brief quotations for review purposes.

Unless otherwise noted, all scripture quotations are taken from the New American Standard Bible®, Copyright © 1960, 1962, 1963, 1968, 1971, 1972, 1973, 1975, 1977, 1995 by The Lockman Foundation. Used by permission. (www.Lockman.org)

Scripture quotations marked "AMP" taken from the Amplified® Bible, Copyright © 1954, 1958, 1962, 1964, 1965, 1987 by The Lockman Foundation Used by permission. (www.Lockman.org)

Scripture quotations marked "GNT" taken from the Good News Translation - Second Edition, Copyright 1992 by American Bible Society. Used by permission.

Scripture quotations marked "KJV" taken from the King James Version of the Bible, public domain.

All references to "Strong's" refer to Strong's Exhaustive Concordance of the Bible, public domain.

Published by WordCrafts Press
Buffalo, Wyoming 82834
www.wordcrafts.net

DEDICATION

This is the seventh book that I have written (including Chewing the Daily Cud Volumes 1—3) and the dedication is to the one who has been a part of my life since 1969 and is still the one who inspires me, encourages me and laughs at my jokes, even when they are not funny. Even when she groans at my jokes, it sounds likes she laughs. This book is dedicated to my wife of 45 years, Brenda Sue Boyd.

As with each book, the co-dedication goes to my son Phillip who, for 28 years—as of the time of this writing—has inspired me to live my faith out loud. I stand back amazed as he continues to grow into a man. I also dedicate this to the woman whom God has brought into his life, his wife, Jamie Boyd. They just celebrated their first anniversary. May they both grow into a man and woman of God.

INTRODUCTION

This book is dedicated to the daily grazing in the field of the Word of God. As we not only graze in this wonderful field, we also ruminate on the Word; and like the cow chewing the cud—one of the many ruminant animals—we ruminate on the feast of this Word. According to Dictionary.com, the word *ruminate* means:

- To chew the cud as a ruminant
- To meditate or muse; ponder
- To chew again over and over
- To meditate over and over; ponder

The *cud* that is being chewed is defined again by Dictionary.com as:

- The portion of food that a ruminant returns from the first stomach to the mouth to chew a second time.
- Partially digested food regurgitated from the first stomach of cattle and other ruminants to the mouth for a second chewing
- To reflect or think over something.

I first discovered the concept of *chewing the cud*, a.k.a. *ruminating*, when I was reading from the book of Joshua.

> "This book of the law shall not depart from your mouth, but you shall meditate on it day and night, so that you may careful to do according to all that is written in it, for then you will make yourself prosperous and then you will have good success."
> (Joshua 1:8 NASB)

The Strong's Exhaustive Concordance of the Bible (*Strong's*) brings out the Hebrew meaning of the word *mediate* as:

MEDITATE: hâgâh (haw-gaw')= to *murmur* (in pleasure or anger); by implication to *ponder:* - imagine, meditate, mourn, mutter, roar, X sore, speak, study, talk, utter. (*Strong's*)

That surely implies that if we want to have prosperity and good success then we must do more than just a cursory reading of the Word of God. I am thinking that this 'prosperity' and 'good success,' in light of the Scriptures, is more than attaining stuff and succeeding in life. For me, biblical prosperity and good success are defined as:

- Prosperity: Having enough to meet my needs with an overflow to meet other's needs.
- Good Success: Accomplishing the purposes of God in my life.

These two things are hinged on me taking the Word of God and:

- Muttering under my breath
- Pondering
- Imaging
- Meditating
- Mourning/Groaning
- Roaring
- Speaking
- Talking
- Uttering

It is my hope that this book of Daily Cud will help you to focus on the Word of God and set you into the motion of meditating and ruminating on the Word of God. That it will be part of the process of renewing your mind by keeping it on the Spirit, where there is life and peace, and off of the flesh, where there is death.

Instead of one, thick book of 365 readings for the year, this devotional will be divided into four volumes of three months' worth each. They will include readings from the Old Testament, the New Testament, Psalms and Proverbs, or—as I like to call them—Pro-Verbs. The length of the readings will vary. Initially, there will be multiple readings from Genesis as we get into the pattern of working through the year with a new book in the pattern. Occasionally, as the Spirit leads, we may go to another book. Hopefully, by the end of the year, we will have gleaned an overview of God speaking to humankind.

Rodney-isms

As you are reading through this collection of devotions, you may come across words or phrases that are new to your vernacular. These are what we call Rodney-isms. Here is a guide for understanding them.

- When we mention the Ruminator Class (Sunday School class) we are talking about a group of people who take the Word of God and begin to meditate or ruminate on it like a cow chews the cud. The cow will eat food, chew it, swallow it through four stomachs and then regurgitated the food back in form of a cud and begin to chew it. They tend to look like they are meditating or ruminating as they chew.
- The word *Pro-Verbs* is taken from the book of Proverbs, one of the books of wisdom in the Old Testament. I wrote a 31-day devotional on the 31 chapters of Proverbs that looks at the teachings of positive action between a father and son. I call these *Pro-Verbs* because Pro = positive and Verb = an action word; thus, Pro-Verbs or Positive-Action.
- When I am talking about a man or a woman, I distinguish between them by calling them *man* or *wo-man*. When I talk about human beings in general, I call them *hu-mans* in keeping with the distinguishing differences.
- *Big S* and *little s* is what I use to distinguish The Holy Spirit (Big

S) from the human spirit (little s). For example, in Genesis we see that the Spirit of God (Big S) was hovering over the dark waters. Later, we see in the book of Proverbs (Pro-Verbs) that the spirit of man (little s) is the lamp of the Lord.

- Whenever you read *satan* or *devil,* I will not capitalize these names because I don't feel they deserve the recognition. While *satan* may be a proper name and is given a capital S in the Bible, I try to make the point that, compared to God—to Whom I give a big G—is much greater than satan, who is known as the god (little g) of this world. (2 Corinthians 4:4) Another aspect of the devil is I call him d-evil. He is evil and again it is just another way I choose not to show respect to him. An interesting little note is that if you turn *evil* around, it spells *live.*

I hope this insight on various Rodney-isms enhances your reading pleasure.

Rodney Boyd
2017

DAY 1
ATTITUDINAL ADJUSTMENT

"Have this attitude in yourselves which was also in Christ Jesus."
(Philippians 2:5)

ATTITUDE/LET THIS MIND: phroneo (fron-eh'-o)=From G5424; to *exercise* the *mind*, that is, *entertain* or *have* a *sentiment* or *opinion*; by implication to *be* (mentally) *disposed* (more or less earnestly in a certain direction); intensively to *interest oneself* in (with concern or obedience): - set the affection on, (be) care (-ful), (be like-, + be of one, + be of the same, + let this) mind (-ed, regard, savour, think. **G5424: phren (frane)**=Probably from an obsolete φράω phraō (to *rein* in or *curb*; the *midrif* (as a *partition* of the body), that is, (figuratively and by implication of sympathy) the *feelings* (or sensitive nature; by extension [also in the plural] the *mind* or cognitive faculties): - understanding. (*Strong's*)

Everyone has an attitude. Some are better than others, in that some have a good attitude while others have a bad attitude. Our attitudes are linked to our mindset. What we think and what we believe is manifest in our words and our actions which reflects our attitudes. We have used a quote throughout this devotional and we will use it again.

> *"Unrestrained thoughts (what we think/our attitude) produces unrestrained words (what we say) resulting in unrestrained actions."*
>
> (Unknown)

I like the way the King James Version put it when it uses the phrase, "Let this mind…" That word 'let' speaks of how our attitudes can be directed by us allowing or letting it happen.

> *"Let this mind be in you, which was also in Christ Jesus"*
> (Philippians 2:5 KJV)

Sometimes there is a resistance to an attitude being changed because it goes against the grain of our flesh. The only way that we can have a mind change is by renewing the mind.

> *"And do not be conformed to this world, but be transformed by the renewing of your mind, that you may be able to prove what the will of God is, that which is good and acceptable and perfect."*
> (Romans 12:2)

RENEW: anakainosis (an-ak-ah'ee-no-sis)=From G341; *renovation:* - renewing. **G341: anakainoo** (an-ak-ahee-no'-o)= to *renovate (to restore to good condition; make new or as if new again; repair; to reinvigorate; refresh; revive):* - renew. (*Strong's*)

This attitudinal adjustment of the mind and developing a new mindset is determined by where you mind is set.

> *"For the mind set on the flesh is death, but the mind set on the Spirit is life and peace, because the mind set on the flesh is hostile toward God; for it does not subject itself to the law of God, for it is not even able to do so; and those who are in the flesh cannot please God."*
> (Romans 8:6-8)

> *"The steadfast of mind Thou will keep in perfect peace because it is stayed on (He trusts in) Thee."*
> (Isaiah 26:3, addition mine)

To have the same attitude that was in Christ Jesus, you must have the same mind as Christ Jesus, because the attitude flows from the mind. As we renew our minds to the Word, we begin to have the mind of Christ.

> *"For who has known the mind of the Lord, that he should instruct Him? But we have the mind of Christ."*
>
> (1 Corinthians 2:16)

Another aspect of this attitudinal adjustment is that it is adjusted by faith. We saw in Romans 8:6-8, that death or life and peace are found in the attitude. The mind set on the flesh has a hostile attitude towards God, but the mind set on the Spirit enters into life and peace and pleases God with no attitude of hostility. Faith comes into the mix because without we cannot please God.

> *"And without faith is it impossible to please Him, for he who comes to God must believe that He is and that He is a rewarder of those who diligently seek Him."*
>
> (Hebrews 11:6)

In Philippians 2:3-8, we see the attitude of Christ which is our template for our attitudinal adjustment.

- Do nothing from selfishness
- Do nothing from empty conceit
- Do everything with humility of mind
- Regard one another as more important than himself
- Do not merely look out for your own personal interests
- Also look for the interest of others
- Although Jesus existed in the form of God, He did not regard equality a thing to be grasped. We did not exist in the form of God, but we have God dwelling within us so we don't need to be grasping our spirituality as a thing to be grasped.
- Empty ourselves

- Take on the form of a bond-servant
- Identify with mankind
- Humble ourselves
- Become obedient to the point of death as we die to ourselves daily and live unto Him.

PRAYER: Father, thank You for Your Word so I can renew my mind to line up with what You are thinking and then do what You, Jesus, did in obedience to the Father and manifesting Your Kingdom and will on earth as it is in heaven to others. Amen.

DAY 2
MARKED INIQUITIES

"If Thou, Lord should mark iniquities, O Lord who could stand?"

(Psalm 130:3)

MARK: shamar (shaw-mar')=A primitive root; properly to *hedge* about (as with thorns), that is, *guard*; generally to *protect, attend to*, etc.: - beware, be circumspect, take heed (to self), keep (-er, self), mark, look narrowly, observe, preserve, regard, reserve, save (self), sure, (that lay) wait (for), watch (-man). (*Strong's*)

INIQUITIES: 'avon 'avon (aw-vone', aw-vone')=From H5753; *perversity*, that is, (moral) *evil:* - fault, iniquity, mischief, punishment (of iniquity), sin. **H5753: 'avah (aw-vaw')**=A primitive root; to *crook*, literally or figuratively: - do amiss, bow down, make crooked, commit iniquity, pervert, (do) perverse (-ly), trouble, X turn, do wickedly, do wrong. (*Strong's*)

Santa Claus has a list and he is checking it twice, he's gonna find out who is naughty or nice, because on December twenty fifth, he is coming to town; or at least that's what the song says.

Sometimes, Christians feel as if they need to keep track of people's sins with a mental list of their iniquities. As soon as someone falls into sin or backslides, out comes the list with another checkmark beside the sinner's name. In 2 Corinthians 5:16-19, we see that when we were sinners/

workers of iniquity, God reconciled us to Himself through Christ. We did not deserve it, but we got it. Then we were given a ministry, without going to a Bible School or Seminary. We were given the ministry of reconciliation. God not only gave us this ministry, but defined exactly what that ministry entailed.

> *"Now all these things are from God, who reconciled us to Himself through Christ, and gave us the ministry of reconciliation, namely, that God was in Christ reconciling the world to Himself, not counting their trespasses against them, and He has committed to us the word of reconciliation."*
> (2 Corinthians 5:18-19)

Marking iniquities and counting trespasses against people is not a God thing but a legalistic man thing.

The people who were approaching Jerusalem to the Temple were singing fifteen Songs of Ascent to worship the Lord. They knew they were sinners needing forgiveness, and knew that the Lord could mark their iniquities (count their trespasses against them), and knew that if He did, they could not stand. In contrast to that, they transition with the word "but."

> *"But there is forgiveness with Thee, that Thou may be feared."*
> (Psalm 130:4)

Thank God for the word "but." Thank God for forgiveness. His forgiveness and true fear lets us to realize His mercy, His love, His redemption.

FORGIVENESS: selıychah (sel-ee-khaw')=From H5545; *pardon:* - forgiveness, pardon. **H5545: salach (saw-lakh')**=A primitive root; to *forgive:* - forgive, pardon, spare. (*Strong's*)

FEAR: yare' (yaw-ray')=A primitive root; to *fear;* morally to *revere;*

causatively to *frighten:* - affright, be (make) afraid, dread (-ful), (put in) fear (-ful, -fully, -ing). (be had in) reverence (-end), X see, terrible (act, -ness, thing). (*Strong's*)

This combination of forgiveness and fear (reverence) of the Lord bring hope.

> "*I wait for the Lord, my soul does wait, and in His Word do I hope. My soul waits for the Lord more than the watchmen for the morning; indeed, more than the watchmen for the morning.*"
> (Psalm 130:5-6)

HOPE: yachal (yaw-chal')=A primitive root; to *wait*; by implication to *be patient, hope:* - (cause to, have, make to) hope, be pained, stay, tarry, trust, wait. (*Strong's*)

Here is the formula for Hope: Forgiveness + Fear of the Lord= Hope.

As they approached Jerusalem and the Temple the people were anticipating with confident expectation (hope) for the coming forgiveness through the coming sacrifices. We can have hope now, knowing that the sacrifice and forgiveness has already been done once for all. Israel was called to hope in the Lord. Why?

- With the Lord there is lovingkindness
- With Him (the Lord) there is abundant redemption
- The Lord will redeem Israel from all his iniquities.

The Good News (the Gospel…the death, burial, resurrection of Jesus) is that He has done the same for you and me.

PRAYER: Lord, thank You that my confident expectation (hope) is underscored by my faith (substance of things not seen) and I am redeemed by the blood of the Lamb. Amen.

DAY 3
FRUIT AND DEEDS

"A man will be satisfied with good by the fruit of his words, and the deeds of a man's hand will return to him."
(Pro-Verbs 12:14)

FRUIT: perıy (per-ee')=From H6509; *fruit* (literally or figuratively): - bough, ([first-]) fruit ([-ful]), reward. **H6509: parah (paw-raw')**=A primitive root; to *bear fruit* (literally or figuratively): - bear, bring forth (fruit), (be, cause to be, make) fruitful, grow, increase. (*Strong's*)

DEEDS/RECOMPENSE: gemul (ghem-ool')=From H1580; *treatment*, that is, an *act* (of good or ill); by implication *service* or *requital*: - + as hast served, benefit, desert, deserving, that which he hath given, recompence, reward. **H1580: gamal (gaw-mal')**=A primitive root; to *treat* a person (well or ill), that is, *benefit* or *requite*; by implication (of *toil*) to *ripen*, that is, (specifically) to *wean*: - bestow on, deal bountifully, do (good), recompense, requite, reward, ripen, + serve, wean, yield. (*Strong's*)

The rock-n-roll band, the Rolling Stones, lamented about the futility of not getting any satisfaction and they underscored it by saying, "No" three times. (*I Can't Get No Satisfaction*)

SATISFACTION: śabaʻ śâbeaʻ (saw-bah', saw-bay'-ah)=A primitive root; to *sate* (to satisfy (any appetite or desire) fully, to fill to excess; surfeit; glut) that is, *fill* to satisfaction (literally or figuratively): - have enough, fill (full, self, with), be (to the) full (of), have plenty of, be satiate, satisfy (with), suffice, be weary of. (*Strong's*)

A man or a wo-man will find true satisfaction by their words (what they speak) and their deeds (what they do). But words and deeds start with what you think. Fruits and deeds can be very positive and very productive, producing a good harvest. But if the seeds of thoughts are bad, then you can expect bad fruit and bad deeds to be manifested and the cause-and-effect is they will receive back like kind.

> *"Death and life are in the power of the tongue, and those who love it will eat its fruit."*
>
> (Pro-Verbs 18:21)

> *"But the fruit of the Spirit is love, joy, peace, patience, kindness, goodness, faithfulness, gentleness, self-control; against such things there is no law."*
>
> (Galatians 5:22-23)

> *"Do not be deceived, God is not mocked; for whatever a man sows, this he will also reap. For the one who sows to his own flesh shall from the flesh reap corruption, but the one who sows to the Spirit shall from the Spirit reap eternal life."*
>
> (Galatians 6:7-8)

> *"Faith without corresponding actions (deeds) is dead."*
>
> (James 2:17, addition mine)

> *"So also faith, if it does not have works (deeds and actions of obedience to back it up), by itself is destitute of power (inoperative, dead).*
>
> (James 2:17/The Amplified Bible)

> *"Unrestrained thoughts (what we think, the seed in the soil of the*

heart) produces unrestrained words (what we speak forth from our minds), resulting in unrestrained actions (deeds based on what we think and say)."

(Unknown)

In one of Jesus' parables about seeds, soil, and sowers (Matthew 13:3-23; Mark 4:1-20; Luke 8:5-15) He speaks of good soil and bad soil which produces of like kind. The seed is good and—depending on dealing with what is in the soil—the harvest will be good or bad. The bottom line of the soil that produces good harvest is that:

- The seed is in good ground
- The people heard the Word
- The heart/soil is honest and good
- The people hold fast
- The people bear word with perseverance/steadfastness

PRAYER: Lord, thank You that *I can get* satisfaction yes, yes, yes! Amen.

DAY 4

THE 21-DAY BATTLE AND THE ISSUED COMMAND

"But the prince of the kingdom of Persia was withstanding me for twenty-one days..."

(Daniel 10:13)

NOTE: *This devotion is a little longer than normal. This may be a morning, noon, and night devotion.*

Have you ever prayed about something and, by the time that the answer came, you have forgotten what you were praying about? Or have you been praying about something and you see no answer and, even worse, what you are praying about gets worse? Do you feel resistance to your prayers and to yourself? There could be a couple of reasons for this, but to differentiate what the problem is, we need to start with ourselves.

The first place I would check is the level of my humility factor. Sometimes what I am feeling and experiencing is opposition from God Himself because I am not humble. Sometimes I get in a rut of expecting God to humble me but that is not the way it works.

"You younger men likewise be subject to your elders; and all of you, clothe yourselves with humility toward one another, for God

is opposed to the proud but gives grace to the humble. Therefore, humble yourself *under the mighty hand of God, that He may exalt you at the proper time, casting all your anxiety upon Him, because He cares for you. Be of sober spirit, be on the alert, you adversary, the d-evil, prowls about like a roaring lion, seeking someone to devour, but resist him, firm in your faith, knowing that the same experiences of suffering are being accomplished by your brethren who are in the world."*

(1 Peter 5:5-9, emphasis mine)

This thing called humility affects you in many areas including:

- Receiving grace (divine influence on your heart manifested in your life)
- Exaltation at the proper time (God is never late; His timing is always proper)
- Ability to cast your anxiety on Him (can't do it if you are proud)
- Increasing sobriety and alertness
- Recognize your enemy/adversary, the d-evil.
- Decreased your chance to be devoured
- Ability to resist the d-evil
- Be firm in your faith

If your prayers are being hindered, another place to check is your relationship with your spouse.

"You husbands likewise, live with your wives in an understanding way, as with a weaker vessel, since she is a woman; and grant her honor as a fellow-heir of the grace of life, so that your prayers may not be hindered."

(1 Peter 3:7)

HINDERED: ekkopto (ek-kop'-to)= to *exscind* (to cut out or off); figuratively to *frustrate:* - cut down (off, out), hew down, hinder. (*Strong's*)

If you don't treat your mate (wife or husband) as a fellow-heir of the grace of life, you will experience hindrance in your prayer life. (Read 1 Peter chapter 2 and 3 for full relationship details)

Now back to the main verse for today that deals with resistance to prayer in Daniel's life and, I am convinced, in yours and mind lives.

Daniel was a praying man. Sometimes he received immediate answers and at other times there was a delay in the answer.

> *"So I (Daniel) gave my attention to the Lord God to seek Him by prayer and supplications with fasting, sackcloth and ashes. And I prayed to the Lord my God and confessed and said…"*
>
> (Daniel 9:3-4)

As he prayed for the people of Israel, Daniel's prayer Modus Operandi (M.O.) was:

- He gave attention to the Lord God
- He sought the Lord
- He prayed (talked to God)
- He supplicated (humble specific things)
- He fasted (starved the flesh)
- He put on sackcloth and ashes (heart of repentance)
- He talked to his (my) God
- He confessed (came into agreement with what God says)

> "Now while I was speaking and praying, and confessing my sin and the sin of my people Israel, and presenting my supplication *before the Lord my God in behalf of the holy mountain of my God,* while I was still speaking in prayer *then the man Gabriel whom I had seen in the vision previously, came to me in* my extreme weariness *about the time of the evening offering. And he gave me instruction and talked*

with me, and said O Daniel, I have now come forth to give you insight with understanding."
(Daniel 9:20-22 emphasis mine)

Daniel was:

- Speaking
- Praying
- Confessing his sin
- Confessing the sin of Israel

Something took place while he was doing these things. Something happened, *"while I was still speaking in prayer."* The angel told Daniel the time frame correlating the prayer and the answer initiated.

> *"At the beginning of your supplications the command was issued (word went out), and I have come to tell you, for you are highly esteemed; so give heed to the message and gain understanding of the vision."*
(Daniel 9:23, addition mine)

Now this is how you want your prayers answered; even before you finished praying things are set into motion. But even with Daniel, things were not always immediate. Daniel again had been praying and mourning for three weeks. Read full details leading up to the encounter in Daniel 10:1-11. The angel explained the 21-day delay. This is a big contrast between immediate answer to prayer "while I was still speaking in prayer."

> *"And he said to me, 'O Daniel, man of high esteem, understand the words that I am about to tell you and stand upright,* for I have now been sent to you.' *And when he had spoken this word to me, I stood up trembling."*
(Daniel 10:11, emphasis mine)

Then he said to me (Daniel 10:12):

- Do not be afraid
- From the first day that you set your heart on understanding this and on humbling yourself before your God
- Your words were heard
- I have come into response to your words.

Just like in the first case Daniel prayed, it was heard, and the command was issued, but now there appears to be a delay. The angelic messenger explained what was going on in Daniel 10:13-14.

- The prince of Persia was withstanding me for 21 days
- Michael, one of the chief angelic princes, came to help me
- For I have been left there with the kings (plural) of Persia.
- Now I have come (after a 21-day conflict) to give you understanding (what Daniel was praying about) of what will happen to your people in the latter days, for the vision pertains to the days yet future.

There is so much to glean from this passage, but we will only say that Daniel was a praying man, like you are a praying man or woman. Daniel had one immediate answer and then, in another time, he had a delayed answer. At times we pray and experience a delay in the timetable of our minds and give up after 20 days, when one more day the battle in the heavenly realm would be won and your answer would be there. The moral of the story is; don't give up, keep standing, the answer is on the way.

That was a long devotion. I hope you have taken time to let this one soak in because sometimes there may be a gap between the prayer and the answer.

PRAYER: Lord, thank You that You have issued the command for the answer. I wait on the Lord, whose timetable is perfect. Amen.

DAY 5
THE PERPETUAL SEEKER

> *"If then you have been raised up with Christ, keep seeking the things above, where Christ is seated at the right hand of God."*
> (Colossians 3:1)

Back in the seventies, we would sing songs straight from the Bible. It was great for spiritual edification and scripture memorization. One song we would sing was be the combination of Galatians 2:20 and Colossians 3:1-3.

> *"I have been crucified with Christ; and it is no longer I who live, but Christ lives in me and the life which I now live in the flesh I live by faith in the Son of God, Who loved me and delivered Himself up for me."*
> (Galatians 2:20)

These verses refer to what is known as the Gospel, the Good News, the D.B.R. (Death, Burial, Resurrection of Jesus…nothing more…nothing less).

This Gospel was what Paul was not ashamed about.

> *"For I am not ashamed of the Gospel, for it (the D.B.R.) is the power (dunamis/dynamic ability) of God for salvation to everyone (the quantifier, the scope of who the salvation is for)*

who believes (the qualifier) to the Jew first (chosen) and also to the Greek/Gentile (all the rest of us)."
(Romans 1:16, addition mine)

When we identify with the work that Jesus did on the cross—as He died in our place as the debt satisfier, the propitiation, the satisfactory substitute of what we owed—we also identify with the burial of the old dead man and also the resurrection from the dead. This is what is being referred to in the phrase, *"If you have been raised up with Christ…"* Here is the pattern in the Galatians and Colossians passages:

- I have been (it is good to be a has been)
- Crucified with Christ (nailed to the cross along with the debt against us)
- It is no longer I who live (this is the spiritual reality of what took place on the cross)
- But Christ lives in me (Christ in you, the hope of glory…we have confident expectation of something other than this world)
- The life which I now live in the flesh (in this land of nitty-gritty on planet Earth)
- I live by faith (the substance, assurance, the confirmation, the title deed of things hoped for, confidently expected, the proof of things we don't see and the conviction of their reality as we perceive as real fact what is not revealed to the senses)
- In the Son of God (in His Death, Burial, Resurrection)
- Who loved me (a noun and a verb of action on the cross)
- And delivered Himself up for me (nobody took His life from Him but He gave it willingly as He was obedient to His Father). Obedience took Him from the cross and love kept Him there.

This identification with the Cross (including the Death, Burial, and Resurrection) is what got us to the point of being raised and seated with Christ. The spiritual fact took place, but we are still on planet Earth; by faith, we can implement a mindset.

- If then you have been raised up (identification with the Risen Christ)
- Keep seeking the things above (His Kingdom and His will as prayed in the Lord's prayer in Matthew 6:10)
- Where Christ is seated at the right hand of God (indication of the finished work as He returned to the Father)
- Set your mind (your choice to take authority of how you think, see, and perceive things)
- On things above (not on earth but in Heaven). I look into heaven and I do not see sickness, disease, poverty, evil, or any of the things on Earth. I don't deny these things, but I do deny their right to rule me. I set my mind on salvation, healing, restoration, deliverance, blessing, prosperity (not under the thumb of poverty).
- For (the reason why I need to be setting my mind on heaven)
- You have died (I have been crucified with Christ)

And your life is hidden with Christ in God (Christ is in me with the hope of glory. I am in Him and hidden with Christ in God. I am surrounded with God goodness)

PRAYER: Lord, thank You so much for surrounding me from the inside out. As long as I stay placed in this position, the enemy has no access to me, only that which I allow. Amen!

DAY 6
COMPOSED AND QUIETED

"Surely I have composed and quieted my soul; like a weaned child rests against (upon) *his mother."*
(Psalm 131:2, addition mine)

SOUL: Nephesh (neh'-fesh*)=*From H5314; properly a *breathing* creature, that is, *animal* or (abstractly) *vitality*; used very widely in a literal, accommodated or figurative sense (bodily or mental): - any, appetite, beast, body, breath, creature, X dead (-ly), desire, X [dis-] contented, X fish, ghost, + greedy, he, heart (-y), (hath, X jeopardy of) life (X in jeopardy), lust, man, me, mind, mortality, one, own, person, pleasure, (her-, him-, my-, thy-) self, them (your) -selves, + slay, soul, + tablet, they, thing, (X she) will, X would have it. **H5314: naphash** (naw-fash')=A primitive root; to *breathe*; passively, to *be breathed* upon, that is, (figuratively) *refreshed* (as if by a current of air): - (be) refresh selves (-ed). (*Strong's*)

SOUL: psuche (psoo-khay')=From G5594; *breath*, that is, (by implication) *spirit*, abstractly or concretely (the *animal* sentient principle only; thus distinguished on the one hand from G4151, which is the rational and immortal *soul*; and on the other from G2222, which is mere *vitality*, even of plants: these terms thus exactly correspond respectively to the Hebrew [H5315], [H7307] and [H2416]: - heart (+ -ily), life, mind, soul, + us, + you. **G5594: psucho** (psoo'-kho)=A primary verb; to *breathe* (*voluntarily* but *gently*; thus differing on the one hand from G4154, which denotes properly a *forcible* respiration; and on the other from the base of G109, which refers properly to an inanimate *breeze*), that is, (by implication of reduction of temperature by evaporation) to *chill* (figuratively): - wax cold. (*Strong's*)

The soul, whether in the Hebrew or in the Greek, is linked to our breath. From the time when God came down and breathed His breath into the nostrils of a formed lump of clay and the cause-and-effect was that lump of clay became a living soul, mankind (and wo-mankind) have been exhaling and inhaling ever since. We don't even have to think about it; we just do it. When we exert ourselves or if we become afraid or anxious, the breath level increases as our souls become troubled.

The word for soul in the Greek "psuche/psoo-khay" is where we get the word "psych." Words like "psychiatrist," "psychologist," and "psycho-somatic" deal with the influence of our mind, our will, and our emotions as it effects our physical being.

When the psalmist sings Psalm 103, he takes control and authority over his soul as he tells it to, *"bless the Lord O my soul and all that is within me, bless His Holy name."* For emphasis, he sings it again, *"bless the Lord O my soul, and forget none* (no not one) *of His benefits."* (Psalm 103:1-2, addition mine)

In this Song of Ascent, the psalmist is expressing *his childlike trust in the Lord* in the face of great matters, or things too difficult for him. He said, *"nor do I involve myself in great matters, or in things too difficult for me."* (Psalm 131:1)

When I find myself, "involving myself" in "great matters" and in "things too difficult for me." I find my mind, my will, my emotions being disturbed and I start breathing heavily and getting more and more anxious as things reel out of control.

I need to learn how to have a childlike faith and press into the Lord like, *"a child resting against his mother."* My soul needs to be like a weaned child within me. Like the psalmist does in Psalms 103, I need to take control over my soul and tell it what to so instead of my soul dictating to me how my emotions should react.

> *"Surely I have* composed *and* quieted *my soul."*
> (Psalm 131:2, emphasis mine)

COMPOSED/BEHAVED: shavah (shaw-vaw')=A primitive root; properly to *level*, that is, *equalize*; figuratively to *resemble*; by implication to *adjust* (that is, counterbalance, be suitable, compose, place, yield, etc.): - avail, behave, bring forth, compare, countervail, (be, make) equal, lay, be (make, a-) like, make plain, profit, reckon. (*Strong's*)

QUIETED: damam (daw-mam')= to *be dumb*; by implication to *be astonished*, to *stop*; also to *perish:* - cease, be cut down (off), forbear, hold peace, quiet self, rest, be silent, keep (put to) silence, be (stand), still, tarry, wait. (*Strong's*)

The next time things become too great or too difficult in your life, and you notice your respiratory system working overtime by breathing harder than normal, take some time and tell your soul to behave and be quiet. Then tell your soul to bless the Lord, praise the Lord, exalt the Lord, and magnify the Lord. We need to take our souls to the Spiritual Obedience School.

PRAYER: Lord, thank You for giving me authority over my mind, my will and emotions. Now I rest in You. Amen.

DAY 7
DEFERRED OR FULFILLED

"Hope deferred makes the heart sick, but desire fulfilled is a tree of life."

(Pro-Verbs 13:12)

HOPE: tocheleth (to-kheh'-leth)=From H3176; *expectation:* - hope. **H3176: yachal** (yaw-chal')=A primitive root; to *wait*; by implication to *be patient, hope:* - (cause to, have, make to) hope, be pained, stay, tarry, trust, wait. (*Strong's*)

HOPE: Elpis (el-pece')=Fromελπω elpo which is a primary word (to *anticipate*, usually with pleasure); *expectation* (abstract or concrete) or *confidence:* - faith, hope. (*Strong's*)

Have you ever lost hope? How did you feel? I know that the spirit of hopelessness prevails throughout the world. Many have been standing in faith with expectations of something taking place in their lives as a result of their prayers.

The longer the prayer goes unanswered, however—the longer that their hope is deferred—the sicker they feel within, to the point of giving up.

DEFERRED: mashak (maw-shak')=A primitive root; to *draw*, used in a great variety of applications (including to *sow*, to *sound*, to *prolong*, to *develop*, to *march*, to *remove*, to *delay*, to *be tall*, etc.): - draw (along, out), continue, defer, extend, forbear, X give, handle, make (pro-, sound) long, X sow, scatter, stretch out. (*Strong's*)

Abraham had a promise of God that he received when he was seventy-five years old. At the ripe old age of one hundred, he still had not received the promise of a child.

How long have you been hoping?

> *"In hope against hope he believed, in order that he might become a father of many nations, according to that which had been spoken (promised), 'So shall your descendants be.'"*
> (Romans 4:18, addition mine)

I have heard the verse paraphrased, "In hope against hope he hoped on."

The bottom line is, just because hope is deferred does not mean that you have to give up. It is linked to keeping on believing, keeping on having faith even if the answer is not revealed to your senses.

> *"Now faith is the substance of things hoped for (confidently expected), the evidence of things not seen (revealed to the senses)."*
> (Hebrews 11:1, addition mine)

Abraham was faced with, "hope deferred" but choose not to allow that deferred hope to make him heart sick. How did he do this? The answer is in Romans 4:19-21.

- He did not become weak in the faith.
- He did not contemplate his own body that was good as dead since he was 100 years old.
- He did not contemplate the deadness of Sarah's womb (her womb was a tomb).
- Yet

- With respect to the promise of God, he did not waver in unbelief.
- He grew strong in faith.
- He gave glory to God.

He was fully assured that what God had promised, God was able to perform.

His desired was fulfilled with the birth of Isaac, which eventually led to the ultimate fulfilment with the birth of Jesus.

In Psalm 37:4, the psalmist lays out how desires of the heart are fulfilled.

> *"Delight yourself in the Lord and He (the Lord) will give you the desires of your heart."*
>
> (Psalm 37:4, addition mine)

Some would say that this thing called "delight" would be some sort of giddy emotion, but it is much more than that.

DELIGHT: ʻ**anag** (aw-nag')=A primitive root; to be *soft* or pliable, that is, (figuratively) *effeminate* or luxurious: - delicate (-ness), (have) delight (self), sport self. (*Strong's*)

The idea of becoming soft or pliable means to be able to yield yourself to the Lord's will. The cause-and-effect of you yielding yourself to the Lord in a soft and pliable way is that He will give you the desires of your heart. Your desires will be fulfilled. When I read this, I think of the Lord planting those desires within us; we line up our delight with those desires; and the cause-and-effect is that He will give us what He planted in us.

If you have been standing in faith but your hope has been deferred based on your timetable, don't give up. Keep hoping, keep believing, keep delighting yourself in the Lord, keep hanging onto His promises.

PRAYER: Lord, thank You that You are the God of 11:59 PM, just before the deadline becomes dead. Lord, help me not to get heartsick and give up at 11:58. Amen.

DAY 8
COME, KNOW, RETURN, AND PRESS

"Come let us return to the Lord…"
(Hosea 6:1)

"So let us know, let us press on to know the Lord…"
(Hosea 6:3)

In the story of Hosea the prophet and his wife, Gomer—who was a harlot—God has given us the ultimate example of a loving Lord who makes provision for the unfaithful wife.

> *"When the Lord first spoke through Hosea, the Lord said to Hosea, 'Go, take to yourself a wife of harlotry, and have children of harlotry; for the land commits flagrant harlotry, forsaking the Lord.'"*
> (Hosea 1:2)

Once again, the chosen people choose to sin and God chooses to allow them to hang themselves in their sin, but also provides a way back to Him. Hosea pleads with them to return to the Lord and to press in to know the Lord. In this, there is a picture of the suffering Messiah.

> *"…He has torn us, but He will heal us; He has wounded us, but He will bandage us. He will revive us after two days; He will raise us up on the third day."*
> (Hosea 6:1-2)

Why would the Lord to this for us? The answer is, *"...that we may live before Him."* (Hosea 6:2)

Back in the 70's and the 80's, I led worship in church, in a campus ministry, and at The Full Gospel Business Men's chapter in my home town. One song we use to sing, "Press On" was based on Hosea 6:3.

> *"So let us know, let us press on to know the Lord, His going forth is as certain as the dawn; and He will come to us like the rain, like the spring rain watering the earth. "*
>
> (Hosea 6:3)

The song "Press On" spoke of pressing on to know the Lord. We could be confident that He would come like the dawn and dew on the grass. Even when my faithfulness had failed, I would become like a cloud dissipating before the sun as I became broken realizing that He would make me whole again. The song encouraged us to return to the Lord.

I don't know if you have ever backslidden away from the Lord but I have. I not only backslid, I slid face forward into my former ways, like a dog return to his vomit. (Pro-Verbs 26:11; 2 Peter 2:22) Whenever I read Hosea or sing the song, "Press On," emotions of coming back to Him, knowing Him, returning and pressing into Him explode in my being.

When we return to the Lord, when we press on to know Him, He will do some things found in Hosea 6:1-2:

- Heal us
- Bandage us
- Revive us
- Raise us up before Him

It all starts with:

- Coming
- Returning
- Knowing

PRAYER: Lord, thank You for keeping the door open for me to return back to You over and over again. Amen.

DAY 9
THE GOD PLEASING WALK

"Finally then, brethren, we request and exhort you in the Lord Jesus, that, as you received from us instruction as to how you ought to walk and please *God (just as you actually do walk), that you may excel still more."*

(1 Thessalonians 4:1, emphasis and addition mine)

WALK/CONDUCT: peripateo (per-ee-pat-eh'-o)= to *tread* all *around*, that is, *walk* at large (especially as proof of ability); figuratively to *live, deport oneself, follow* (as a companion or votary): - go, be occupied with, walk (about). (*Strong's*)

PLEASE: aresko (ar-es'-ko)= (through the idea of *exciting* emotion); to *be agreeable* (or by implication to seek to be so): - please. (*Strong's*)

There is an expectancy in this scripture to walk in a certain way and, when you do walk that way, you will be pleasing God. Paul is not just suggesting that this would be a good idea, but there is an urgency of emotions in that, not only did he request you to walk and please God, but to also please Him in your walk.

REQUEST/BESEECH: erotao (er-o-tah'-o)= to *interrogate*; by implication to *request*: - ask, beseech, desire, intreat, pray. (*Strong's*)

EXHORT: parakaleo (par-ak-al-eh'-o)= to *call near*, that is, *invite, invoke* (by *imploration, hortation* or *consolation*): - beseech, call for, (be of good) comfort, desire, (give) exhort (-ation), intreat, pray. (*Strong's*)

Pleasing God is impossible unless you have faith in your walk.

> "*But without faith is it impossible to please and be satisfactory to Him. For whoever would come near to God must [necessarily] believe that God exists and that He is the rewarder of those who earnestly and diligently seek Him [out].*"
> (Hebrews 11:6 The Amplified Bible)

If you are walking without faith you cannot: (1) please God, or (2) walk as you ought to walk. The walk in this case is based on the commandments that Paul had given to the readers by the authority of the Lord Jesus. The nature of this walk of faith for their sanctification is found in 1 Thessalonians 4:3-6:

- Abstain from sexual immorality: IMMORALITY: porneia (por-ni'-ah)= From G4203; *harlotry* (including *adultery* and *incest*); figuratively *idolatry:* - fornication. G4203: porneuō (porn-yoo'-o)=From G4204; to *act* the *harlot*, that is, (literally) *indulge* unlawful *lust* (of either sex), or (figuratively) *practice idolatry:* - commit (fornication). G4204: pornē (por'-nay)= a *strumpet*; figuratively an *idolater:* - harlot, whore. (*Strong's*)
- Each knows how to possess his own vessel in sanctification and honor: POSESS: ktaomai=ktah'-om-ahee= A primary verb; to *get*, that is, *acquire* (by any means; *own*): - obtain, possess, provide, purchase. (*Strong's*)
- Not in lustful passion like the Gentiles who do not know God: LUSTFUL PASSION:=epithumia *(ep-ee-thoo-mee'-ah)*=From G1937; a *longing* (especially for what is forbidden): - concupiscence, desire, lust (after). G1937: epithumeō (ep-ee-thoo-meh'-o)= to set the *heart upon,* that is, *long* for (rightfully or otherwise): - covet, desire, would fain, lust (after). (*Strong's*)

- No man transgress and defraud his brother in the matter: TRANSGRESS: huperbainō (hoop-er-bah'ee-no)= to *transcend*; that is, (figuratively) to *overreach:* - go beyond (known limits, my emphasis) DEFRAUD: pleonekteō (pleh-on-ek-teh'-o)= From G4123; to *be covetous*, that is, (by implication) to *over reach:* - get an advantage, defraud, make a gain. G4123: pleonektēs (pleh-on-ek'-tace)=*holding (desiring) more*, that is, *eager for gain* (*avaricious*, hence a *defrauder*): - covetous. (*Strong's*)

The bottom line is that God has called us for purpose. The purpose is not impurity, but the calling is for the purpose of sanctification.

SANCTIFICATION: Hagiasmos (hag-ee-as-mos')=From G37; properly *purification*, that is, (the state) *purity*; concretely (by Hebraism) a *purifier:* - holiness, sanctification. **G37: hagiazo** (hag-ee-ad'-zo)=From G40; to *make holy*, that is, (ceremonially) *purify* or *consecrate*; (mentally) to *venerate:* - hallow, be holy, sanctify. **G40: hagios** (hag'-ee-os)=From αγος hagos (an *awful* thing) compare G53, [H2282]; *sacred* (physically *pure*, morally *blameless* or *religious*, ceremonially *consecrated*): - (most) holy (one, thing), saint. (*Strong's*)

PRAYER: Lord, thank You that I have a calling and I have purpose, and both involve walking by faith and pleasing You. Thank You, Lord, that I can excel in both my calling and my purpose in You. Amen.

DAY 10
A DWELLING PLACE

"Until I find a place for the Lord, a dwelling place for the Mighty One of Jacob."

(Psalm 132:5)

"God is spirit, and those who worship Him must worship in spirit and truth."

(John 4:24)

When Jesus was crossing into the land of Samaria, He once again bucked the religious system by going to an area where the religious people hated the inhabitants, the Samaritans. When a Jew was traveling and they came to the borders of Samaria, they would cross over the river, go around the land, and then cross back over in their journey.

Jesus did not cross the river but went straight into the heart of the land, to a place called Sychar. There Jesus not only interacted with the people of the land, but in particular, He interacted with a woman, who not only was a female, she was an immoral woman.

After initial conversation, she figured out that Jesus was a prophet, and her conversation shifted to matters of worship. (John 4:1-19) She spoke of her forefathers worshipping in the mountain in Samaria, while *you people* said that Jerusalem is the place where men out to worship. (John 4:20)

WORSHIP: proskuneo (pros-koo-neh'-o)= (meaning to *kiss*, like a dog *licking* his masters hand); to *fawn* or *crouch to*, that is, (literally or figuratively) *prostrate* oneself in homage (*do reverence* to, *adore*): - worship. (*Strong's*)

Wow, things have not changed much since then. People argue that we should come into large cathedrals, in homes, in school auditoriums, in brick and mortar edifices, under tabernacles, in municipal auditoriums, in mega churches, temples, synagogues, on the golf course and any other place you would gather people in large or small gatherings. The woman at the well questions Jesus about the proper place of worship.

> *"Jesus said to her, 'Woman, believe Me, an hour is coming when neither in this mountain, no in Jerusalem, shall you worship the Father.'"*
>
> (John 4:21)

The psalmist is searching for, "a dwelling place" for the Mighty One of Jacob. Of course, God is a Spirit and a mere mortal is a poor place to house the Creator of the Universe.

> *"You worship that which you do not know; we worship that which we know; for salvation is from the Jews. But an hour is coming, and now is, when the true worshipers shall worship the Father in spirit and truth, for such people the Father seeks to be His worshipers. God is spirit; and those who worship Him must worship in spirit and truth.*
>
> (John 4:22-24)

The location of worship appears to not be of mortar, but of mortal being. This worship appears to take place now not on one mountain or the other, but in a place called "spirit" and it done in "truth."

SPIRIT: Pneuma (pnyoo'-mah)= a *current* of air, that is, *breath* (*blast*) or a *breeze*; by analogy or figuratively a *spirit*, that is, (human) the rational *soul*, (by implication) *vital principle*, mental *disposition*, etc., or (superhuman) an *angel*, *daemon*, or (divine) God, Christ's *spirit*, the Holy *spirit*: - ghost, life, spirit (-ual, -ually), mind. (*Strong's*)

TRUTH: aletheia (al-ay'-thi-a)=From G227; *truth:* - true, X truly, truth, verity. **G227: alethes** (al-ay-thace')= *true* (as *not concealing*): - true, truly, truth. (*Strong's*)

This place of worship is to be within our own being, invisible to the eye, but just as concrete and real as the places that we gather to worship the Lord. In the day of the psalmist, tabernacles, temples, and stone and mortar were utilized to come and worship the Lord. Now our bodies are places where we can worship the Lord 24 hours, seven days a week, 365 days a year.

> *"Now may the God of peace Himself sanctify you entirely; and may your spirit and soul and body be preserved complete, without blame at the coming of our Lord Jesus Christ."*
> (1 Thessalonians 5:23)

> *"The spirit of man is the lamp of the LORD, Searching all the innermost parts of his being."*
> (Pro-Verbs 20:27)

> *"Do you not know that you are a temple/sanctuary and that the Spirit of God dwells in you? If any man destroys the temple/sanctuary of God, God will destroy him, for the temple of God is holy, and that is what you are."*
> (1 Corinthians 3:16-17, addition mine)

> *"Or do you not know that your body is a temple/sanctuary of the Holy Spirit who is in you, whom you have from God and that you are not your own? For you have been bought with a price;*

therefore, glorify God in your body."
(1 Corinthians 6:19-20, addition mine)

When the Holy Spirit (Big S) dwells in your human spirit (little s) and your mind is renewed by the truth (The Word), as man says, "Yes Lord," worship takes place. No longer do we have to search the world for a place to worship the Lord, because we are that place.

We worship in an attitude and a place called the spirit. We worship in truth that the Lord (as the Word) in His prayer to the Father when He prayed that we would be sanctified by truth and then defined Truth, *"Thy Word is Truth."*

PRAYER: Thank You, Lord, that You chose flesh and blood (the moral) to allow people to worship You. You did not to limit Yourself to stone/brick/concrete (mortar) for me to meet with You. Thank You that You are in my spirit (little s) and Your Word is my truth. Amen.

DAY 11
THE WRONG-RIGHT WAY

"There is a way that seems right unto a man, but its end is the way of death."
                    (Pro-Verbs 14:12; Pro-Verbs 16:25)

The singer/songwriter Paul Anka wrote a song made famous by Frank Sinatra and Elvis Presley that bragged about living their life their way

A man becomes convinced that what they are doing is *the right way*. It just seems right and nothing anyone can do will convince them otherwise. I am the same way. I don't get up in the morning and make a conscious decision to go the way of wrong. I rationalize that what I do either is right or that the rules don't apply to me and I am immune from the consequence of my wrong actions that am convinced they are right. I never consider the end result of my actions. The effect of my cause will reveal whether I was right or wrong.

The righteous man (the one who does right) does exist. One aspect of this righteous man is not that he does it *his* way but that he does it *His* way. This righteous man walks under ordered steps by the Lord.

"The steps of the righteous man are ordered by the Lord."
                                        (Psalm 37:23)

GOOD/RIGHTEOUS: Geber (gheh'-ber)=From H1396; properly a *valiant* man or *warrior*, generally a *person* simply: - every one, man, X mighty. H1396: gâbar *(gaw-bar')*=A primitive root; to *be strong*; by implication to *prevail, act insolently*: - exceed, confirm, be great, be mighty, prevail, put to more [strength], strengthen, be stronger, be valiant. (*Strong's*)

On one hand, there is *none righteous,* and on the other hand we are, *the righteous*. What changes between Romans 3:10 and 2 Corinthians 5:21? Well whatever it is, it is not what seems right to the man.

> *"As it is written, there is none righteous, none."*
>
> (Romans 3:10)

RIGHTEOUSNESS: Dikaios (dik'-ah-yos)=From G1349; *equitable* (in character or act); by implication *innocent, holy* (absolutely or relatively): - just, meet, right (-eous). (*Strong's*)

> *"He made Him who knew no sin to be sin on our behalf, so that we might become the righteousness of God in Him."*
>
> (2 Corinthians 5:21, emphasis mine)

What bridges the gap of being righteous (right) and unrighteousness (wrong) is the Cross of Christ.... the Gospel of Christ...the D.B.R. (Death, Burial, and Resurrection...nothing more...nothing less).

> *"For I (Paul) am not ashamed of the Gospel (D.B.R.) for it (the Gospel) is the power of God, for salvation to everyone (whosoever) who believes (that Jesus is raised from the dead and confesses Jesus as Lord), to the Jew first and also to the Greek."*
>
> (Romans 1:16, addition mine)

Now how is this righteousness revealed? How can we know that our way is not right and that His way is right?

> *"For in it (the Gospel...the D.B.R.) the righteousness (right way)*

of God (not my seemingly right way) is revealed from faith to faith; as it is written, but the righteous man shall live by faith."
(Romans 1:17; Habakkuk 2:4; Galatians 3:11; Hebrews 10:38, addition mine)

I have heard that the center pole of a tent is called the standard. It is to this standard that all guidelines are attached and staked into the ground. This standard (pole) is to me a perfect picture of being righteous (right). If we attach our life guidelines to our standard (what seems right), there will be an instability in our life to the point of death or destruction.

PRAYER: Father, forgive me for living and walking in my own self-considered right way. Help me to attach my life lines to Your standard. Amen.

DAY 12
THE LORD OF THE POURED

"And it will come about after this that I will pour out my Spirit on all mankind..."

(Joel 2:28)

"...but this is what was spoken of through the prophet Joel, 'and it shall be in the last days,' God says, 'that I will pour forth of My Spirit upon all mankind...'"

(Acts 2:16-17; Joel 2:28)

There is a promise of *a pouring*, and what will be *poured* out is God's Spirit. The coverage of this *pouring* will be upon *all mankind*...not just a select few.

The Spirit was with God in the beginning, in the creation, as The Spirit was hovering, sweeping over, and moving upon the dark depths.

"In the beginning God created the heavens and the earth. And the earth was formless and void, and darkness was over the surface of the deep; and the Spirit of God was moving (hovering/sweeping) over the surface (waste and emptiness) of the waters."

(Genesis 1:1-2, addition mine)

SPIRIT: ruach (roo'-akh**)**=From H7306; *wind*; by resemblance *breath*, that is, a sensible (or even violent) exhalation; figuratively *life, anger,* *unsubstantiality*; by extension a *region* of the sky; by resemblance *spirit*, but only of a rational being (including its expression and functions): - air, anger, blast, breath, X cool, courage, mind, X quarter, X side, spirit ([-ual]), tempest, X vain, ([whirl-]) wind (-y).(*Strong's*)

When God formed a lump of clay, and then breathed His breath into the nostrils, the lump of clay became a living soul.

BREATHED: naphach (naw-fakh')=A primitive root; to *puff*, in various applications (literally, to *inflate, blow* hard, *scatter, kindle, expire*; figuratively, to *disesteem*): - blow, breath, give up, cause to lose [life], seething, snuff. (*Strong's*)

BREATH: neshamah (nesh-aw-maw')=From H5395; a *puff*, that is, *wind*, angry or vital *breath*, divine *inspiration, intellect* or (concretely) an *animal:* - blast, (that) breath (-eth), inspiration, soul, spirit. **H5395: nasham (naw-sham')**=A primitive root; properly to *blow* away, that is, *destroy:* - destroy. (*Strong's*)

The cause-and-effect of the Spirit in creation of the world, and creation of the first human being, was good and life.

Throughout the Old Testament, the Holy Spirit is evident in everything from filling artistic craftsman, to prophets anointing kings, to prophets proclaiming the Word of God for the present and the future. Then He (the person of the Holy Spirit) breaks into the New Testament with the Holy conception of Jesus, anointing at His baptism, with Him in times of temptation in the wilderness, and as He came out of the wilderness experience.

He was full of the Spirit, and went about for three years doing good and healing all who were oppressed by the d-evil because He was anointed with the Holy Spirit and power. He passed on this Holy Spirit by His breath and then told His followers to wait in Jerusalem after His death for the pouring of the Holy Spirit so they could be His witnesses. And now the Holy Spirit is in all who say that, "Jesus is Lord."

The Holy Spirit has been poured out and has never left. He still lives in and flows in people's lives and still is on all flesh to convict people of the truth so they can come into intimate relationship with the Father, Son and yes, the (not a) Holy Ghost/Spirit.

PRAYER: Father, thank You for the connection with You via Your *poured out* Holy Spirit and my human spirit. Amen.

DAY 13
OCCUPY WITH A DISCIPLINED LIFE

"For even when we were with you, we used to give you this order: if anyone will not work, neither let him eat."

(2 Thessalonians 3:10)

"And he called his ten servants, and delivered them ten pounds, and said unto them, 'Occupy till I come.'"

(Luke 19:13)

OCCUPY: Pragmateuomai (prag-mat-yoo'-om-ahee)=From G4229; to *busy oneself* with, that is, to *trade*: - occupy. **G4229: pragma** (prag'-mah)=From G4238; a *deed*; by implication an *affair*; by extension an *object* (material): - business, matter, thing, work. **G4238: prasso** (pras'-so)=A primary verb; to practise, that is, *perform repeatedly* or *habitually* (thus differing from G4160, which properly refers to a *single* act); by implication to *execute*, *accomplish*, etc.; specifically to *collect* (dues), *fare* (personally): - commit, deeds, do, exact, keep, require, use arts. (*Strong's*)

In Paul's first letter to those in Thessalonica, he wrote to them about their hope of the return of the Lord. In his second letter to them, he addresses some concerns about their misunderstanding what he had said about the return of the Lord. Some had taken what he had said and had stopped working and began to live an undisciplined life.

"For we hear that some among you are leading an undisciplined

> *life, doing no work at all but acting like busybodies."*
> (2 Thessalonians 3:11)

Paul wrote this letter in 52 A.D.; Jesus has not returned at the time of this writing in 2017, but we still look for His return. When Jesus left planet Earth, He had given instructions to wait for the Holy Spirit, Who was poured out so that they could be witnesses.

> *"And after He had said these things, He was lifted up while they were looking on, and a cloud received Him out of their sight. And as they were gazing intently into the sky while He was departing, behold two men in white clothing stood beside them; and they also said, 'Men of Galilee, why do you stand looking up in the sky? This Jesus, who has been taken up from you into heaven, will come in just the same way as you have watched Him go into heaven.'"*
> (Acts 1:9-11)

The Acts passage was written in 60-62 A.D., and in 52 A.D., people were still looking into the sky in an undisciplined manner. If those two men clothed in white had shown up, they might have said, "Men of Thessalonica, why do you wait around for the Lord to come back and not working?"

Sometimes we get into the rut of waiting and forget that life goes on where we live. We get lazy and undisciplined in our walk with the Lord, and leech off others who not only are waiting for the Lord's return, but have realized that life goes on. Paul spoke to the church in Thessalonica and left them an example for them to follow.

> *"For you yourselves know how you ought to follow our example, because we did not act in an undisciplined manner among you."*
> (2 Thessalonians 3:7)

Discipline covers many areas of our lives as we wait for His return.

> *"But have nothing to do with worldly fables fit only for old women. On the other hand,* discipline yourself for the purpose

of godliness; for bodily discipline is only of little profit, but godliness is profitable for all things, since it holds promise for the present life and also for the life to come."
(1 Timothy 4:7-8, emphasis mine)

This "life to come" is when the Lord returns. Until then, there is a "present life" that we are to be disciplined in until He returns. Until He returns, Paul encourages them on how to live the disciplined versus the undisciplined life. This includes:

- Allow the Lord to direct your hearts into the love of God and into the steadfastness of Christ.
- Keep aloof from every brother who leads and unruly (undisciplined) life.
- Walk in the traditions that were received from Paul.
- Pay for bread you eat.
- Work with labor and hardship.
- Keep working night and day.
- Don't be a burden to anyone.
- Work so you can eat.
- Lead a discipline life by working.
- Don't act like a busybody.
- Work in quiet fashion.
- Eat your own bread.
- Do not grow weary of doing good.
- Don't associate with the man who is undisciplined (to put him to shame).
- *Yet,* with the one you do not associate, *do not regard him as an enemy,* but admonish him as a brother.

PRAYER: Lord, as I wait for Your return, show me how to be disciplined and an encourager to the undisciplined. Maranatha, come quickly Lord. Amen.

DAY 14

THE COMMANDED BLESSING

"...for there the Lord commanded the blessing—life forever more."

(Psalm 133:3)

This song of ascent—that is a song sung as the people approach the Temple for the purpose of sacrifice and worship—is an picture of dwelling together in unity.

"Behold, how good and how pleasant it is for brother to dwell together in unity!"

(Psalm 133:1)

GOOD: tob (tobe)= *good* (as an adjective) in the widest sense; used likewise as a noun, both in the masculine and the feminine, the singular and the plural (*good*, a *good* or *good* thing, a *good* man or woman; the *good*, *goods* or *good* things, *good* men or women), also as an adverb (*well*): - beautiful, best, better, bountiful, cheerful, at ease, X fair (word), (be in) favour, fine, glad, good (deed, -lier, liest, -ly, -ness, -s), graciously, joyful, kindly, kindness, liketh (best), loving, merry, X most, pleasant, + pleaseth, pleasure, precious, prosperity, ready, sweet, wealth, welfare, (be) well ([-favoured]). (*Strong's*)

PLEASANT: naʻıym (naw-eem')=From H5276; *delightful* (objectively or subjectively, literally or figuratively): - pleasant (-ure), sweet. **H5276:**

na'ıym (naw-eem')=A primitive root; to *be agreeable* (literally or figuratively): - pass in beauty, be delight, be pleasant, be sweet. (*Strong's*)

I like that Psalm 133:1 ends with an exclamation point. When brothers are divided and live (if you can call it living) bad and in unpleasantness, it really is miserable. Jesus spoke of this in His sermon about the Kingdom given on the mountain.

> *"If therefore you are presenting your offering at the altar, and there remember that your brother has something against you, leave your offering there before the altar, and go your way; first be reconciled to your brother, and then come and present your offering."*
>
> (Matthew 5:23-24)

In verse two, we see that this dwelling together in unity is related to anointing with oil upon the head. The anointing of oil, the pouring out and rubbing into and smearing upon, has multiple purposes. Anointing oil is used for designating—or consecrating—someone or something for the purpose of the Lord's work. It is also used for *refreshing* after a long journey and can be medicinal in nature.

Today, when we anoint someone, we take a little drop of oil and place it on the forehead. In the days of the Song of Ascents, it was a little more free-flowing; a cruse of oil that was mixed with various herbs and fragrances was poured out liberally on the head of the one being anointed. The flow of oil would travel from the head, down upon the beard, and down to the edges of the robe.

Now that is a lot of goodness and pleasantry flowing. That represents unity from the top of the head to the soles of the feet.

UNITY: gam (gam)=By contraction from an unused root meaning to *gather*; properly *assemblage*; used only adverbially *also, even, yea, though*;

often repeated as correlation *both... and:* - again, alike, also, (so much) as (soon), both (so) . . . and, but, either . . . or, even, for all, (in) likewise (manner), moreover, nay . . . neither, one, then (-refore), though, what, with, yea. (*Strong's*)

This flowing of oil is pictured with a natural object that the people of that day had seen many times with the snow-capped mountains of Mount Hermon. As the snow melts, there is a flow of water to the valley that feeds into the headway of the Jordan River. It is within this flow of unity that the Lord commanded the blessing. What was the blessing commanded? It was life forever more. So it is when we dwell together in unity. We experience the blessing of life, and that more abundantly.

BLESSING: berakah (ber-aw-kaw')=From H1288; *benediction*; by implication *prosperity:* - blessing, liberal, pool, present. **H1288: barak** (baw-rak')=A primitive root; to *kneel*; by implication to *bless* God (as an act of adoration), and (vice-versa) man (as a benefit); also (by euphemism) to *curse* (God or the king, as treason): - X abundantly, X altogether, X at all, blaspheme, bless, congratulate, curse, X greatly, X indeed, kneel (down), praise, salute, X still, thank. (*Strong's*)

LIFE: Chay (khah'ee)=From H2421; *alive*; hence *raw* (flesh); *fresh* (plant, water, year), *strong*; also (as noun, especially in the feminine singular and masculine plural) *life* (or living thing), whether literally or figuratively: - + age, alive, appetite, (wild) beast, company, congregation, life (-time), live (-ly), living (creature, thing), maintenance, + merry, multitude, + (be) old, quick, raw, running, springing, troop. **H2421: chayah** (khaw-yaw')=A prim root to *live*, whether literally or figuratively; causatively to *revive:* - keep (leave, make) alive, X certainly, give (promise) life, (let, suffer to) live, nourish up, preserve (alive), quicken, recover, repair, restore (to life), revive, (X God) save (alive, life, lives), X surely, be whole. (*Strong's*)

This blessing, the prosperity of the abundance of being alive is spoken of by Jesus as it is by being in Him and Him in use that we can ever be truly in unity.

> *"The thief cometh not, but for to steal, and to kill, and to destroy: I am come that they might have life, and that they might have it more abundantly."*
>
> (John 10:10 KJV)

How long will the blessed abundant life last? Forever! Forever is a long time, like an eternity.

FOREVER: ʻolam ʻolam **(**o-lawm', o-lawm')= properly *concealed*, that is, the *vanishing* point; generally time *out of mind* (past or future), that is, (practically) *eternity*; frequentative adverbially (especially with prepositional prefix) *always*: - always (-s), ancient (time), any more, continuance, eternal, (for, [n-]) ever (-lasting, -more, of old), lasting, long (time), (of) old (time), perpetual, at any time, (beginning of the) world (+ without end). (*Strong's*)

PRAYER: Lord, thank You so much for Jesus Who came that we can live in unity around Him; and not only have life after death, but have abundant life now and forever more. Amen.

DAY 15
THE NATURE OF THE STRIFE STIRRER

"A hot-tempered man stirs up strife, but the slow to anger pacifies contention."

(Pro-Verbs 15:18)

There is nothing new under the sun, according to Solomon in his infinite wisdom.

"That which has been is that which will be, and that which has been done is that which will be done. So, there is nothing new under the sun."

(Ecclesiastes 1:9)

I would be remiss to say that there is something new under the *Son*.

"Therefore, if any man is in Christ (the Son), *he is a new creation, the old things passed away, behold new things have come."*
(2 Corinthians 5:17, addition and emphasis mine)

Solomon is correct when he points out that there is nothing new under the sun, especially mankind's emotions that came into being with the fall.

HOT-TEMPERED/WRATHFUL: chemah chema' (khay-maw', khay-maw')= *heat;* figuratively *anger, poison* (from its *fever*): - anger, bottles, hot displeasure, furious (-ly, -ry), heat, indignation, poison, rage, wrath (-ful). (*Strong's*)

The first aspect of the "strife stirrer" is the undercurrent of anger which is a poison that gives that man a fever that will not be satisfied unless there is strife among people. This stirring of strife is the great disturber of unity among the brethren.

STRIFE: madon (maw-dohn')=From H1777; a *contest* or quarrel: - brawling, contention (-ous), discord, strife. **H1777: dıyn dun (deen, doon)**=A primitive root (compare H113); to *rule*; by implication to *judge* (as umpire); also to *strive* (as at law): - contend, execute (judgment), judge, minister judgment, plead (the cause), at strife, strive. (*Strong's*)

Have you ever been around someone who is constantly stirring the pot of contention? They are miserable people who want to make all around them miserable. The answer to this Strife Stirrer is the Anger Pacifier. It will take someone who is slow to anger. James speaks of this person.

> *"This you know, my beloved brethren. But let everyone be quick to hear, slow to speak and slow to anger; for the anger of man does not achieve the righteousness of God."*
> (James 1:19-20)

You can't fight fire with fire or anger with anger. Jesus spoke of the Anger Pacifier in the Sermon on the Mount as He spoke of the Blessings of Beatitudes (the attitude that we need to BE having).

> *"Blessed are the peacemakers, for they shall be called sons of God."*
> (Matthew 5:9)

These peacemakers will pacify contentions.

PACIFY: shaqat (shaw-kat')=A primitive root; to *repose* (usually figuratively): - appease, idleness, (at, be at, be in, give) quiet (-ness), (be at, be in, give, have, take) rest, settle, be still. (*Strong's*)

PEACEMAKERS: **eirenopoios** (i-ray-nop-oy-os')= *pacificatory*, that is, (subjectively) *peaceable:* - peacemaker. (*Strong's*)

The only way that we can bring people to a state of quietness and rest, and to bring peace into a situation, is not negotiations and deals between two parties. They must be introduced to the Prince of Peace.

> "For a child will be born to us, a son will be given to us; and the government will rest on His shoulders; and His name will be called Wonderful Counselor, Mighty God, Eternal Father, Prince of Peace."
>
> (Isaiah 9:6)

This child was born; grew in wisdom and stature; was obedient to His Father in baptism; and for three years demonstrated the Kingdom and Will of God on earth as it is in Heaven. He (Jesus) was, and is, the Wonderful Counselor Who in fact was the Mighty God Who was and is the Eternal Father. Yes, this Jesus was and is The Prince of Peace and not strife.

PRAYER: Father, thank You that we can be Strife Calmers as we introduce the Prince of Peace into situations. Amen.

DAY 16
THE GOOD SEEKERS

"Seek good and not evil, that you may live; and thus may the Lord God of hosts be with you just as you have said."
(Amos 5:14)

The northern kingdom of Israel is under the pronouncement of judgment by a shepherd and someone who cultivated sycamore trees. The judgment was falling on deaf ears because of the prosperity in the land. The heartbeat for God for these rebellious people is that they would live and not die. That is why a prophet is raised up to proclaim the problem, declare the solution, and to call them to seeking the Lord.

God chose someone who was not a hired gun. God chose someone who had not been to the University of Prophets at good old U.O.P. He was not a man who would profit by being a prophet. I appreciate those who have been to school to become proficient in the Word of God and become a minister who is worthy of his hire, but God is not limited to professional ministers.

Thus is the case with Brother Amos.

*"Then Amos answered and said to Amaziah, 'I am not a prophet, nor am I the son of a prophet; for I am a herdsman and a grower/*nipper/cultivator *of sycamore figs/trees.'"*
(Amos 7:14, addition and emphasis mine)

Within chapter five of Amos, there are three urgings for the people to "seek the Lord."

SEEK: darash (daw-rash')=A primitive root; properly to *tread* or *frequent*; usually to *follow* (for pursuit or search); by implication to *seek* or *ask*; specifically to *worship:* - ask, X at all, care for, X diligently, inquire, make inquisition, [necro-] mancer, question, require, search, seek [for, out], X surely. (*Strong's*)

I like the idea that this seeking is, "specifically to worship." This explains that what is to be worshipped is the Lord Himself. Much too often, I find myself seeking and worshiping someone or something other than the Lord.

- Seek Me that you may live (Amos 5:4)
- Seek the Lord that you may live (Amos 5:6)
- Seek good and not evil, that you may live (Amos 5:14)

The cause-and-effect of this seeking is that you may live.

LIVE: chayah (khaw-yaw')=A prim root to *live*, whether literally or figuratively; causatively to *revive:* - keep (leave, make) alive, X certainly, give (promise) life, (let, suffer to) live, nourish up, preserve (alive), quicken, recover, repair, restore (to life), revive, (X God) save (alive, life, lives), X surely, be whole. (*Strong's*)

Jesus spoke of this seeking in regard to things.

> *"But seek (continually seek) first (not as an afterthought) His (not yours) Kingdom (a place where the King rules) and His righteousness (His standard of right); and all these things (stuff) shall be added (not subtracted) unto you."*
> (Matthew 6:33, addition mine)

> *"But seek for (aim at and strive after) first of all His kingdom,*

and His righteousness (His way of doing and being right), and then all these things taken together will be given you besides."
(Matthew 6:33 The Amplified Bible)

SEEK: zeteo (dzay-teh'-o)=Of uncertain affinity; to *seek* (literally or figuratively); specifically (by Hebraism) to *worship* (God), or (in a bad sense) to *plot* (against life): - be (go) about, desire, endeavor, enquire (for), require, (X will) seek (after, for, means). (*Strong's*)

"Keep on asking and it will be given you; keep on seeking and you will find; and keep on knocking [reverently] and the door will be opened to you. For everyone who keeps on asking receives, and to him who keeps on seeking finds and to him who keeps on knocking it will be opened."
(Matthew 7:7-8, addition mine)

PRAYER: Lord, forgive me for not seeking Your ways, for not seeking good, but for seeking evil. Lord, thank You that, as I seek You and Your good, I will and have found life. Amen.

DAY 17
THE MUZZLED OX RELEASED

"For the Scripture says, 'You shall not muzzle the ox while he is threshing', and 'The laborer is worthy of his wages/hire.'"
(1 Timothy 5:18, addition mine)

A *muzzle* is defined in Dictionary.com as:

a device, usually an arrangement of straps or wires, placed over an animal's mouth to prevent the animal from biting, eating, etc. To muzzle and animal is defined as: to put a muzzle on (an animal or its mouth) so as to prevent biting, eating, etc.

The context of this statement is in relationship to elders who rule well over people as being considered *worthy of double honor* and especially those who work hard at *preaching and teaching*. The implication is to not withhold finances from those who provide services to us.

In the natural world, if a plumber comes to fix your leak, you cannot expect him to be paid with a thank you. If you go into a market and filled your basket with food, if you pushed your cart out without paying, you would be stopped at the door. If you have someone build a house you cannot expect to move in and shut the door in the builder's face. Why? Because a laborer (someone who provides you services) is worthy of their hire.

Well, what about this ox?

OX: bous (booce)=Probably from the base of G1006; an *ox* (as *grazing*), that is, an animal of that species ("beef"): - ox. **G1006: bosko** (bos'-ko)= to *pasture*; by extension to *fodder*; reflexively to *graze*: - feed, keep. (*Strong's*)

The ox is laboring by threshing out the corn. If the ox is not fed by being muzzled, the ox grows weak, and cannot perform at optimum level.

THRESH/TREAD: aloao (al-o-ah'-o)=From the same as G257; to *tread* out grain: - thresh, tread out the corn. G257: halōn (*hal'-ohn*)= a threshing *floor* (as *rolled* hard), that is, (figuratively) the *grain* (and chaff, as just threshed): - floor. (*Strong's*)

The threshing floor was utilized as a tool to take wheat (or grains) and separate the fruit of the wheat from the chaff (the husks that surrounds the fruit). At times, the fruit of the wheat and the chaff were gathered together and thrown in the air which would blow and separate the two. Then chaff was collected and burned.

The use of oxen in the process of the thrashing began by putting the sheaves of wheat on the threshing floor. The oxen were used to either walk on the sheaves; or they were attached to the grinding wheel (large stone) which would crush the sheaths of wheat as it turned as they walked.

The oxen need their strength for either method. If you muzzle the ox, you end up having to use a longer process for threshing.

> *"Where no oxen are, the manger is clean, but much revenue comes by the strength of the ox."*
>
> (Pro-Verbs 14:4)

Where no oxen are…there is no food in the manger (feeding trough) and no dung in the stall or field. But when you do not muzzle the ox you get two things: (1) cow dung (2) good production on the threshing floor which will bring in more money.

This reference about the ox is about those elders who rule well.

> *"Let the elders who rule well be considered worthy of double honor, especially those who work hard (in the Word) at preaching and teaching."*
>
> (1 Timothy 5:17, addition mine)

Sometimes, people expect their leaders to be kept humble by keeping them poor; but the exact opposite should be done. Don't muzzle those of double honor by paying them poorly. Give them what is due them.

> *"And let the one who is taught the Word share all good things with him who teaches."*
>
> (Galatians 6:6)

You might have a full-time pastor or staff of pastors who get a salary. You might have someone who is not on staff, but teaches and preaches and feeds you the Word of God. Show them some honor, yes in salary, but also in kindness; little gifts throughout the year; an *'atta boy* pat on the back; take them out to eat; or a gift here and there. They really are worthy of your honor.

PRAYER: Lord, forgive me for muzzling those who feed me the Word of God. Show me some way that I can take the muzzle off the ox Amen.

DAY 18
THE NIGHT WATCHERS

"Behold, bless the Lord, all servants of the Lord, who serve by night in the house of the Lord!"

(Psalm 134:1)

The "night watchers" are those who stand guard at night over a walled city watching enemies. According to the Holman Illustrated Bible Dictionary (Holman Bible Publishers 2003) a night watch is an "ancient division of time." In the Jewish culture the night was divided into three watches including: (1) evening (2) mid-night (3) morning. The fourth watch was just before dawn.

"For a thousand years in Your sight are like yesterday when it passes by, or as a watch in the night."

(Psalm 90:4)

"My eyes anticipate the night watches, that I may meditate on Your Word."

(Psalm 119:148)

"Arise, cry aloud in the night, at the beginning of the night watches; Pour out your heart like water before the presence of the Lord; Lift up your hands to Him For the life of your little ones, who are faint because of hunger at the head of every street."

(Lamentations 2:19)

> *"Therefore, be on the alert—for you do not know when the master of the house is coming, whether in the evening, at midnight, or when the rooster crows, or in the morning."*
>
> (Mark 13:35)

> *"And in the fourth watch of the night He came to them, walking on the sea."*
>
> (Matthew 14:25)

> *"Seeing them straining at the oars, for the wind was against them, at about the fourth watch of the night He came to them, walking on the sea; and He intended to pass by them."*
>
> (Mark 6:48)

The night speaks of a dark time and also speaks of the fact that the Lord is a *24-hour Savior,* and worthy of prayer, praise, worship all of the time.

Notice in the night that blessings were flowing back and forth during the night watch.

> *"Lift up your hands to the sanctuary, and bless the Lord. May the Lord bless you from Zion, He who made heaven and earth."*
>
> (Psalm 134:2-3)

BLESS: barak (baw-rak')=A primitive root; to *kneel*; by implication to *bless* God (as an act of adoration), and (vice-versa) man (as a benefit); also (by euphemism) to *curse* (God or the king, as treason): - X abundantly, X altogether, X at all, blaspheme, bless, congratulate, curse, X greatly, X indeed, kneel (down), praise, salute, X still, thank. (*Strong's*)

Another Psalm speaks of the night and declarations about the Lord.

> *"It is good to give thanks to the Lord, and to sing praises to Thy name, O Most High, to declare Thy lovingkindness in the*

morning *and Thy faithfulness by* night."
(Psalm 92:1-2, emphasis mine)

PRAYER: Lord, thank You that You have got me covered morning, noon, and night. I choose to bless You during *all watches*. Amen.

DAY 19

THE GLORY CROWN

"A gray head is a crown of glory; it is found in the way of righteousness."

(Pro-Verbs 16:31)

I was looking at some pictures of my wife Brenda and me back in our youth. We were young, vibrant, active, and we had heads of hair minus the gray.

I am just excited that I still have a full head of hair now. I also used to have a full beard—minus gray hair—but over time the beard progressively became gray/white. My beard went from a distinguished salt and pepper to full white/gray of Santa Claus proportions. The hair is starting to follow the pattern.

I have never dyed my hair nor beard but I have thought about it. After much agonizing, Brenda decided to stop coloring her hair; and she looks *fabulous*. She gets many compliments about her choice; some say it even makes her look younger. Some have said that, when they saw how good she looks, they were encouraged to quit dying their hair.

Gray hair is found throughout the Bible and is always considered a sign of wisdom, honor, and respect. Some would say that gray/white hair is a sign of worry, but not so. According to our verse in Pro-Verbs, this crown of glory is found somewhere.

"…it is found in the way of righteousness."
(Pro-Verbs 16:31)

RIGHTEOUSNESS: tsedaqah (tsed-aw-kaw')=From H6663; *rightness* (abstractly), subjectively (*rectitude*), objectively (*justice*), morally (*virtue*) or figuratively (*prosperity*): - justice, moderately, right (-eous) (act, -ly, -ness). **H6663: tsadaq** (tsaw-dak')=A primitive root; to *be* (causatively *make*) *right* (in a moral or forensic sense): - cleanse, clear self, (be, do) just (-ice, -ify, -ify self), (be, turn to) righteous (-ness). (*Strong's*)

Here are a few of the verses.

> *"Even to your old age I will be the same, and even to your graying years I will bear you! I have done it, and I will carry you; and I will bear you and I will deliver you. To whom would you compare Me and make Me equal and compare Me, that we would be alike?"*
> (Isaiah 46:4-5, emphasis mine)

> *"Even when I am old and gray, do not forsake me, my God, till I declare Your power to the next generation, Your mighty acts to all who are to come. Your righteousness, God, reaches to the heavens, You who have done great things. Who is like you, God?"*
> (Psalm 71:18-19)

> *"A king will remain in power as long as his rule is honest, just, and fair. We admire the strength of youth and respect the gray hair of age."*
> (Pro-Verbs 20:28-29, GNT)

> *"Show respect for old people and honor them. Reverently obey me; I am the Lord."*
> (Leviticus 19:32, GNT)

PRAYER: Lord, help me to live up to my hair color, according to Your wisdom. Amen.

DAY 20
RECIPROCITY PROMISED

"For the day of the Lord draws near on all the nations. As you have done, it will be done to you. Your dealings will return on your own head."

(Obadiah 1:15)

Obadiah is one chapter that is packed with insight and wisdom about cause-and-effect. Yahweh's servant, Obadiah, speaks with a prophetic revelation of the cause-and-effect of Edom rising up against Judah/Jerusalem because they did not come to the aid of Judah. Instead, they assisted their Babylonian captors' pillaging of Jerusalem and ratting out the refugees.

God has knowledge of, and will deal with, the enemies of Judah as He deals with:

- Pride
- Deceit
- Human wisdom
- Conspiracy

While on the surface it appears that in Edom's eyes that they will escape judgment, they did not factor in the, *"day of the Lord"* where judgment comes for the nations and deliverance comes for God's people. This is where the cause-and-effect principle comes in for Edom.

"For the day of the Lord draws near on all nations. As you have done, it will be done to you. Your dealings will return on your own head."
(Obadiah 1:15)

- Sinners will receive payback that is just.
- The God of deliverance will deliver with holiness.
- There will be a Restoration Remnant.
- Bottom line ... It is God's Kingdom that they have been against.

The cause-and-effect of God's move is hinged on the lament and grief, in the form of passionate prayer to God. They came to the One Who could judge, save, and correct their situation.

When we go through stuff, the quicker we repent and lament, the quicker God will move on our behalf. We must realize that, *"the day of the Lord"* is near. It reminds me of when anxiety, worry, fear, doubt, and the tensions of life are swirling around our hearts and our minds.

Paul encourages us to:

"Let your forbearing spirit (controlled) be known to all men."
(Philippians 4:5)

The reason for this confidence in the face of what we are experiencing is found at the end of the verse.

"The Lord is near."
(Philippians 4:5)

The psalmist speaks of this same principle in Psalm 37 as they are encouraged to:

> *"Fret not yourself because of evildoers, be not envious toward wrongdoers."*
>
> (Psalm 37:1)

Why? Because the cause-and-effect will eventually take place.

> *"For they (evildoers and wrongdoers like Edom) will wither quickly like the grass and fade like the green herbs."*
>
> (Psalm 37:2, addition mine)

PRAYER: Lord, help me keep my eye on You, knowing that You have and will do what needs to be done. Amen.

DAY 21
THE GOOD FIGHT

"I have fought the good fight, I have finished the course, I have kept the faith; in the future there is laid up for me the crown of righteousness, which the Lord, the righteous Judge, will award to me on that day; and not only me, but also to all who have loved His appearing."

(2 Timothy 4:7-8)

The end is coming near for Paul, and he writes encouragement to his son in the faith, Timothy, to not give up. He likens this walk of faith as a fight and encourages Timothy to persevere and to fight a good fight as opposed to a bad fight. At some point, God/Jesus is to judge the living and the dead and Timothy is encouraged to continue the fight.

In 2 Timothy 4, these are some things Timothy should be doing, and really the things that we should all be doing as we fight the good fight of faith.

- Preach the Word: to *herald* (as a public *crier*), especially divine truth (the gospel): - preach (-er), proclaim, publish.
- NOTE: This does not mean that we should all get a theological degree and preach from a pulpit. We all can proclaim the Death, Burial, and Resurrection.
- Be ready in season and out of season: (1) to *stand upon*, that is, *be present* (in various applications, friendly or otherwise, usually

literally): - assault, come (in, to, unto, upon), be at hand (instant), present, stand (before, by, over). (2) *opportunely:* - conveniently, in season. (3) *inopportunely:* - out of season.

- NOTE: No matter where you go, no matter who is surrounding you, we should be ready when it is convenient and when it is not necessarily a good opportunity.
- Reprove: to *confute, admonish:* - convict, convince, tell a fault, rebuke, reprove.
- NOTE: When someone is at fault about something, admonish, and not only let them know they are wrong, but tell them how they could be right.
- Rebuke: to *tax upon*, that is, *censure* or *admonish*; by implication *forbid:* - (straitly) charge, rebuke.
- NOTE: Sometimes we need to be bold enough to let people know they are wrong and you may need to be stronger in the correction.
- Exhort: to *call near*, that is, *invite, invoke* (by *imploration, hortation* or *consolation*): - beseech, call for, (be of good) comfort, desire, (give) exhort (-ation), intreat, pray
- Doing all of these things with great patience and instruction: (1) *longanimity*, that is, (objectively) *forbearance* or (subjectively) *fortitude:* - longsuffering, patience. (2) *instruction* (the act or the matter): - doctrine, hath been taught.
- Be sober in all things: to *abstain* from wine (*keep sober*), that is, (figuratively) *be discreet:* - be sober, watch.
- Endure hardships: to *undergo hardship:* - be afflicted, endure afflictions (hardness), suffer trouble.
- Do the work of an evangelist: (1) *toil* (as an effort or occupation); by implication an *act:* - deed, doing, labour, work. (2) a *preacher* of the gospel: - evangelist.

Fulfill your ministry: (1) to *carry* out *fully* (in evidence), that is, *completely assure* (or *convince*), *entirely accomplish:* - most surely believe, fully know (persuade), make full proof of. (2) *attendance* (as a servant, etc.); figuratively (eleemosynary) *aid*, (official) *service* (especially of the Christian teacher, or technically of the *diaconate*): - (ad-) minister (-ing, -tration, -try), office, relief, service (-ing).

PRAYER: Lord, thank You for giving the ability and insight on how to fight the good fight. Now it is up to me to utilize those techniques and I will. Amen.

DAY 22
HANDY MAN'S WORK

"The idols of the nations are but silver and gold, the work of man's hand."

(Psalm 135:15)

Idols are images made as a tangible object to direct worship towards. These inanimate, man-made objects are poor substitutes compared to the Living God. In Romans, Paul speaks of those who have:

"exchanged the glory of the incorruptible God for an image…"
(Romans 1:23)

As a result of their misguided worship, the wrath of God was revealed. (Romans 1:18) There are two things revealed: (1) The Gospel (2) God's wrath.

"For in it (Death, Burial, Resurrection, aka the Gospel) the righteousness of God is revealed from faith to faith; as it is written, but the righteous man shall live by faith."
(Romans 1:17, addition and emphasis mine)

"For the wrath of God is revealed from heaven against all ungodliness, and unrighteousness of men who suppress the truth in unrighteousness of men, who suppresses the truth in

unrighteousness, because that which is known of God is evident within them; for God made it evident to them."
>(Romans 1:18-19 emphasis mine)

These people refused to give honor to Him as God or give thanks to God and became futile in their speculations and their darkened, foolish hearts. The wise guys (and gals) became fools. Instead of worshiping God, they worshipped themselves in images in the form of corruptible man, birds, four-footed animals, and crawling creatures. (Romans 1:22-23) The idols of the nations were:

- Made of silver and gold
- The works of man's hands
- Have mouths but do not speak
- Have ears but do not see
- Have no breath at all in their mouths

Those who make and worship these lifeless idols will be like them. (Psalm 115:1-8) When you make and worship lifeless idols that you will be like, in reality you trust them and not the real deal, the Living God Who speaks, sees, and has the Spirit Breath flowing out of Him. When we worship Him, we will be like Him.

PRAYER: Father, You Sir are the real deal. I worship You and thank You that I am created in Your image, and after the fall, I am being changed daily into Your image again. Amen.

DAY 23
TESTED HEARTS

"The refining pot is for silver and the furnace for gold, but the Lord tests the hearts."

(Pro-Verbs 17:3)

TESTS: bachan (baw-khan')=A primitive root; to *test* (especially metals); generally and figuratively to *investigate:* - examine, prove, tempt, try (trial). (*Strong's*)

When you have heart problems, you go through a series of tests to determine what the problem may be. One of these tests is a stress test.

"Stress tests are tests performed by a doctor and/or trained technician to determine the amount of stress that your heart can manage before developing either an abnormal rhythm or evidence of ischemia (not enough blood flow to the heart muscle). The most commonly performed stress test is the exercise stress test."

(Web MD)

When you test metals, the piece of metal is placed under extreme pressure to see where the breaking point might occur.

Silversmiths and goldsmiths test and refines those precious metals by putting them under heat/fire. As the temperature rises, the impurities—called dross—floats to the top. The dross is skimmed away until you have pure silver and gold. God is in the business of checking out our hearts.

> *"Sheol (the nether world) and Abaddon (destruction), lie open before the Lord, how much more the hearts of men!"*
> (Pro-Verbs 15:11, addition mine)

The psalmist gives the Lord an open invitation to examine and test him.

> *"Examine me, O Lord and try me; test my mind and my heart."*
> (Psalm 26:2)

The Lord Himself defines Who He is: The searcher of the hearts.

> *"I, the Lord search the heart I test the mind, even to give to each man according to his ways, according to the results of his deeds."*
> (Jeremiah 17:10)

One day the Lord will return for some refining and purifying of offerings, that they may be presented to Him in righteousness and then they (the offerings) will be pleasing to the Lord.

> *"But who can endure the day of His coming? And who can stand when He appears? He is like a refiner's fire and like fullers (laundrymen's) soap. And He will sit as a smelter and purifier of silver, and He will purify the sons of Levi and refine them like gold and silver, so that they may present to the Lord offerings in righteousness. Then the offering of Judah and Jerusalem will be pleasing to the Lord, as in the days of old and as in former years."*
> (Malachi 3:2-4, addition mine)

This testing, this pressure upon your faith by various trials, will produce endurance which will lead to a perfect result, that you may be perfect and complete and lacking in nothing.

> *"Consider it all joy, my brethren, when you encounter various trials, knowing that the testing of your faith produces endurance. And let (allow) endurance have its perfect result, that you may be perfect and complete, lacking in nothing."*
> (James 1:2-4, addition mine)

Sometimes I find that I am lacking in something. During those times, I may need to see how I have allowed the testing of my faith to do its work.

While we are here on planet Earth, we are to conduct ourselves in a certain way. How we conduct ourselves under the pressures and testing of the Lord will be the difference from abundant life to a futile way.

> *"So then, my beloved, just as you have always obeyed, not as in my presence only, but now much more in my absence, work out your own salvation with fear and trembling; for it is God Who is at work in you, both to will and to work for His good pleasure. Do all things without grumbling or disputing (complaining)."*
> (Philippians 2:12-14, addition mine)

> *"...conduct yourselves in fear during the time of your stay upon earth; knowing that you were not redeemed with perishable things like silver or gold from your futile way of life inherited from your forefathers, but with the precious blood, as of a lamb unblemished and spotless, the blood of Christ."*
> (1 Peter 1:17-19)

PRAYER: Lord, thank You for testing me, examining me, purifying, and refining me. Thank You, Lord, for the blood of Jesus and His Death, Burial, and Resurrection that will deal with anything that You find in me that takes me from unrighteousness to being the righteousness of God in Christ. Amen.

DAY 24
GOD'S HOLY APPOINTMENT BOOK

"But God appointed a worm when dawn came the next day, and it attacked the plant and it withered."

(Jonah 4:7)

Jonah was a prophet with an attitude. God speaks to him; Jonah hears God; instead of obeying, he chooses to run from the presence of God. (Jonah 1:1-3)

PRESENCE: panıym (paw-neem')=the *face* (as the part that *turns*) (*Strong's*)

"Repent therefore and return, that your sins may be wiped way in order that times of refreshing may come from the presence of the Lord."

(Acts 3:19)

PRESENCE: prosopon (pros'-o-pon)=*visage*; from the *front* (as being *towards view*), that is, the *countenance, aspect, appearance, surface*; by implication *presence, person:* - (outward) appearance, X before, countenance, face, fashion, (mens) person, presence. (*Strong's*)

Being face to face with God, because that is where God wants you to be, is where there is refreshing. The only reason to run from the Presence of God is that your sin stands with you. When you repent and return—with your sins wiped away—that opens the door for times of refreshing to come. That refreshing is found in the Presence of the Lord.

In this story, Jonah ran. He boarded a ship going in the opposite direction from where God wanted him to go. A great storm came. Jonah told the captain of the ship that the storm was due to his rebellion and to throw him overboard. The captain didn't want to, but finally agreed; Jonah was thrown overboard. Jonah was caught by a great fish. Jonah was thrown up by the great fish.

Finally, God had Jonah's attention. The good news is that the Word of the Lord came to Jonah, *"the second time."* This time Jonah listened and obeyed. He went and preached to the people of Nineveh. The people of Nineveh *"believed in God; and they called a fast and put on sackcloth from the greatest to the least of them."* They repented, returned, their sins were wiped away, and times of refreshing came from the Presence of the Lord. (Jonah 3:1-10)

God turned and relented (repented) and withdrew His burning anger so that Nineveh would not perish. Now Jonah had another problem. You would think that Jonah would have a Hallelujah good time; however, it was just the opposite.

> *"But it greatly displeased Jonah, and he became angry."*
> (Jonah 4:1)

Jonah became suicidal and asked the Lord to kill him. The Lord responds with a question.

> *"And the Lord said, 'Do you have good reason to be angry?'"*
> (Jonah 4:4)

God now books Jonah in *His Holy Appointment Book*. There were three appointments that God used to teach Jonah a lesson.

- A plant (Jonah 4:5)
- A worm (Jonah 4:7)
- A scorching east wind and sun (Jonah 4:8)

God appointed a plant to grow over Jonah's head to shade him from the sun and deliver him from discomfort. Jonah was extremely happy about the plant. Then God appointed a worm and it attacked the thing that made Jonah very happy and the plant withered. As Jonah was exposed, God appointed a scorching east wind and the sun beat down on Jonah's head. It was as if Jonah was in a confection oven with the heat swirling and baking him like cookie. Jonah became faint and begged with all his soul to die. (Jonah 4:6-8)

> *"Death is better to me than life."*
>
> (Jonah 4:8)

Now that God had Jonah's attention through His holy appointments, God asks the same question that He previously asked.

> *"And the Lord said, 'Do you have a good reason to be angry?'"*
>
> (Jonah 4:4)

> *"Then God said to Jonah, 'Do you have a good reason to be angry, about the plant?' 'I have a good reason to be angry, even to death?'"*
>
> (Jonah 4:9)

The Lord then explains His holy appointments in reference to Nineveh.

- You had compassion on the plant for which you did not work.
- You did not cause the plant to grow.
- The plant came up overnight and perished overnight.
- Should I not have compassion on Nineveh, the great city?
- There were more than 120,000 persons who know not the

difference between their right and left hand, as well as many animals.

Nothing else is heard from Jonah or God on the matter. The question is, "are you in the middle of His holy appointment? Are you on the run from His refreshing presence? Are you angry because those who don't deserve His mercy or grace are getting it?

PRAYER: Lord, forgive men for wishing Your wrath to come on people. Lord may Your Word take root in their lives and may they repent. I repent now. Amen.

DAY 25

YES INDEED...IN DEED

"They profess to know God, but by their deeds they deny Him, being detestable and disobedient, and worthless for any good deed."

(Titus 1:16)

NOTE: We have covered Titus two other times in the "Daily Cud" books, and there is an interweaving of the thought about deeds. Once again, we speak of deeds and their relationship with our walk with the Lord. At first, I thought there was no need to cover deeds again; but I was impressed (I feel by the Lord) that I needed to hear this again, and just maybe someone else needs to also.

In Titus 3:5, we are told that our salvation is, *"not on the basis of deeds which we have done in righteousness."*

DEEDS: Ergon (er'-gon)=From εργω ergo (a primary but obsolete word; to *work*); *toil* (as an effort or occupation); by implication an *act:* - deed, doing, labour, work. (*Strong's*)

The companion verse is found in the book of Ephesians.

"For by grace you have been saved through faith; and that not of yourselves, it is the gift of God; not as a result of works (deeds/ ergon), *that no one should boast for we are His workmanship,*

> *created in Christ Jesus for good works* (deeds/ergon), *which God prepared beforehand, that we should walk in them."*
>
> (Ephesians 2:8-10, emphasis mine)

While Titus 3:5 and Ephesians 2:8-10 tell us that deeds do not help us in our salvation, we are also encouraged to walk in deeds. In the New American Standard version of the Bible, the word *deeds* is listed a total of 9 times in Titus. In Ephesians, we are told that salvation is not by deeds, but that we were to walk in prepared deeds.

People sometimes profess to know God but their deeds tend to deny God. The characteristics of the people and their deeds are:

- They profess to know God.
- By their deeds they deny God.
- Their deeds are detestable, disobedient, and worthless.

Young men were encouraged to show themselves as:

- Example of good deeds (Titus 2:7)
- Examples of purity in doctrine (Titus 2:7)
- Dignified (Titus 2:7)
- Sound speech beyond reproach (Titus 2:8)

Just doing good deeds does not necessarily mean that we are good. We must be redeemed.

> *"...who gave Himself for us, that He might redeem us from every lawless deed and purify for Himself a people for His own possession, zealous for good deeds."*
>
> (Titus 2:14)

Paul later encourages Titus:

- Be zealous for good deeds (Titus 2:14)
- Be ready for every good deed (Titus 3:1)

- Be careful to engage in good deeds (Titus 3:8)
- Learn to engage in good deeds (Titus 3:14)
- Meet pressing needs by your deeds (Titus 3:14)

PRAYER: Lord, I thank You that deeds can't save me but sure can keep me on track with what I am supposed to be doing after salvation. Amen.

DAY 26
EVERLASTING LOVINGKINDNESS:
LAWD HAVE MERCY

"Give thanks to the Lord, for He is good; for His lovingkindness is everlasting."

(Psalm 136:1)

One of the criticisms of today's modern praise and worship songs is that they are repetitive. They say the same thing over and over and over again. Well, add the psalmist into that mix of musical proponents of God's lovingkindness.

The phrase *"for His lovingkindness is everlasting"* appears within the 26 verses in Psalm 136 for a total of 26 times. Hmmm, I wonder what the psalmist is trying to say?

You would think that he would come up with a little more creativity in his praise and worship music. Surely saying it one time would be sufficient to get his thoughts across.

LOVINGKINDNESS/MERCY: chesed (kheh'-sed)=From H2616; *kindness*; by implication (towards God) *piety*; rarely (by opprobrium) *reproof,* or (subjectively) *beauty:* - favour, good deed (-liness, -ness), kindly, (loving-) kindness, merciful (kindness), mercy, pity, reproach, wicked thing. **H2616: chasad** (khaw-sad')=A primitive root; properly perhaps to *bow* (the neck only (compare H2603) in courtesy to an equal), that is, to *be kind*; also (by euphemism (compare H1288), but rarely) to *reprove:* - shew self merciful, put to shame. (*Strong's*)

The concept of everlasting is a long time. His mercy is eternal, everlasting, forever, does not run out. *Wow!*

EVERLASTING: 'olam 'olam (o-lawm', o-lawm')=From H5956; properly *concealed*, that is, the *vanishing* point; generally time *out of mind* (past or future), that is, (practically) *eternity*; frequentative adverbially (especially with prepositional prefix) *always*: - always (-s), ancient (time), any more, continuance, eternal, (for, [n-]) ever (-lasting, -more, of old), lasting, long (time), (of) old (time), perpetual, at any time, (beginning of the) world (+ without end). **H5956: 'alam** (aw-lam')=A primitive root; to *veil* from sight, that is, *conceal* (literally or figuratively): - X any ways, blind, dissembler, hide (self), secret (thing). (*Strong's*)

The good news is that there is not—and will not—be a depletion of God's mercy in our lives. That is what the weeping prophet was saying in the midst of his lamenting.

> "*The Lord's lovingkindness indeed never ceases; for His compassions never fail, they (mercy and compassion) are new every morning; great is Thy faithfulness.*"
> (Lamentations 3:22-23, addition mine)

The psalmist speaks again of this lovingkindness.

> "*Because Your lovingkindness is better than life, my lips will praise You. So I will bless You as long as I live; I will lift up my hands in Your name. My soul is satisfied as with marrow and fatness, and my mouth offers praises with joyful lips.*"
> (Psalm 63:3-5)

The psalmist seems to have a one-track mind (not really) with this lovingkindness thing.

> *"It is good to give thanks to the Lord, and to sing praises to Thy name, O Most High; to declare Thy lovingkindness in the morning, and thy faithfulness by night."*
>
> (Psalm 92:1-2)

Let us look at what excites the psalmist in Psalm 136 that he would use that phrase, *"For His lovingkindness* (mercy) *is everlasting."*

- He (God) is good.
- He is the God of Gods.
- He is the Lord of Lords.
- He alone does great wonders.
- He made the heavens with skill.
- He spread out the earth above the waters.
- He made the great lights.
- He made the sun to rule by day.
- He made the moon and stars to rule by night.
- He smote the Egyptians in their first-born.
- He brought Israel out from their midst.
- He used His strong hand and outstretched arm.
- He divided the Red Sea asunder.
- He made Israel pass through the midst of it (the Red Sea).
- He overthrew Pharaoh and his army in the Red Sea.
- He led His people through the wilderness.
- He smote great kings.
- He slew mighty kings.
- He slew Sihon, king of the Amorites.
- He slew Og, king of Bashan.
- He gave their land as a heritage.
- He gave their land to Israel, His servant.
- He remembered us in our low estate.

- He has rescued us from our adversaries.
- He gives food to all flesh.
- He is the God of Heaven.

God was faithful, showed His love and His mercy to Israel. Through Jesus the Christ—the Anointed One—He is just as faithful to you and me. His mercy is still in the everlasting mode and continues. Maybe we can start a list of our own about why His lovingkindness is everlasting.

PRAYER: Lord, You have shown Your everlasting mercy to me. Help me to show Your mercy to those in my life. Amen.

DAY 27
THE HAND OF THE TONGUE

> *"Death and life are in the power of the tongue, and those who love it will eat its fruit."*
>
> (Pro-Verbs 18:21)

The tongue, compared to the other parts of the body, is a relatively small part of the body. According to James, it is small, but boasts great things.

> *"So also the tongue is a small part of the body, and yet it boasts of great things…"*
>
> (James 3:5)

James then speaks of our ability to tame the tongue.

> *"But no one can tame the tongue…"*
>
> (James 3:8a)

Why can this small part of the body not be tamed?

> *"…it is a restless evil and full of deadly poison."*
>
> (James 3:8b)

Pro-Verbs 18: 1speaks of a man who quarrels against all sound wisdom, who separates himself from others, and who seeks his own desire. A picture is painted of a fool and the power that even a fool holds in his mouth. Here are some of the strokes of the fool painted in Pro-Verbs:

- He separates himself.
- He seeks his own desire.
- He quarrels against all sound wisdom.
- He does not delight in understanding.
- He delights only in revealing his own mind.
- He is a wicked man who brings contempt.
- He shows partiality to the wicked (not good).
- He thrusts aside the righteous in judgment.
- His lips bring strife.
- His mouth calls for blow (strikes).
- His lips are the snare for his soul.
- His whispering words are like dainty morsels.
- His words go down into the innermost parts of the body.
- He is slack in his work.
- He is a slacker whose brother is a destroyer.
- He does not run into a strong tower but runs into a manmade "strong city."
- He has a high wall (of pride) of imagination.
- His heart is haughty.
- He gives answers before he hears which results in folly and shame.
- He has a broken spirit and cannot endure sickness.
- His pleading of his case at first seem just until it is examined.
- He is easy to be offended but can offend and is harder to be one than a strong city.
- His contentions are like the bars of a castle.

This portrait of a fool is not a pretty picture. It is the fruit, or speech, of a man's mouth that will satisfy him. Man will be satisfied with the product of his lips. (Pro-Verbs 18:21) This is where we came in on our daily devotion.

> *"Death and life are in the power (hand) of the tongue, and those who love it will eat its fruit."*
>
> (Pro-Verbs 18:21, addition mine)

This power is for the fool and it is also for the wise man. The cause-and-effect will either be death (for the fool) or life (for the wise man).

Whatever this Pro-Verb is about, this one thing I know; when seeds are sown, fruit is born. It will be positive or negative fruit of our mouth and what we speak will either be death or life.

PRAYER: Lord, help me to be aware of when I am eating and speaking deadly fruit. May the fruit of my lips bring life to me and to all whom I speak to or about. Amen.

DAY 28

THE SEA OF SINS

"He will again have compassion on us; He will tread our iniquities under foot, yes, Thou wilt cast all their sins into the depths of the sea."

(Micah 7:19)

Once again, another prophet is pronouncing judgement on the Southern Kingdom and the Northern Kingdom of Israel. The book of Micah opens with encouragement for the reader to "hear," "listen," and let/allow the Lord to "be a witness" against them.

Yes, they were in rebellion; and yes, there is cause-and-effect. But the biggest *yes* is what God intends to do in the end of the book. This is the same *yes* that we can rely upon: His mercy; His forgiveness; His redemption; His love to flow towards us also. What will the Great Shepherd of the flock do for them and us? Let's check out Micah 7:14-19 for some more insight.

- He will shepherd the people with His scepter the flock of His possession.
- We will be in the midst of a fruitful field.
- We will feed like the days of old (before rebellion).
- We will see miracles like when coming out of the bondage of Egypt.
- He will show us miracles.

- Other nations will see and be ashamed of all our might.
- Other nations will put their hand on their mouth.
- Other nations ears will be deaf.
- Other nations will lick the dust like a serpent, like reptiles of the earth.
- Other nations will come trembling out of their fortresses.
- Other nations will be afraid before Him.
- He pardons our iniquities.
- He passes over the rebellious act of the remnant of His possession.
- He does not retain His anger forever.
- He delights in unchanging love.
- He will again have compassion on us.
- He will tread our iniquities underfoot.
- He will cast all our sins into the depths of the sea.

I don't know about you, but if He has done all of that for Israel…for you…for me, I for one am not going to try to act as if it is not true. If my iniquities have been treaded under His foot and my sins cast into a sea, I am not going to try to get them back from under His feet and go deep-sea fishing for my forgiven sins.

PRAYER: Lord, thank You for restoration. Amen.

DAY 29

SONIC LOVE/FAITH

"I thank my God always, making mention of you in my prayers, because I hear of your love, and of the faith which you have toward the Lord Jesus, and toward all the saints."
                                    (Philemon 1:4-5)

Sound waves travel. When people hear about the way you love people and how your faith is toward Jesus—and not toward what you pray for—that gets their attention.

Paul was prisoner; of Jesus and literally in prison in Rome. The sound waves of the people's love toward Jesus and others broke through the prison walls to Paul's ears. This love emanated from the house of Philemon, including Apphia (wife) and Archippus (son). Hey, not much of a mega church, but a church just the same

Onesimus was a runaway slave who had travelled from Colosse. He had found his way into Paul's presence in Rome. Apparently, Paul had led Onesimus down the Romans Road To Salvation. **NOTE:** the R.R.T.S. is not a real road but leads you to a place more real than Rome. It leads you into the presence of God. This is a series of verses found in the Book of Romans. It is not the only method of leading someone to the Lord, but it worked for me.

Back in 1970, my girlfriend—who would later become my wife—led me down the Romans Road To Salvation. It changed my life. She even led me in a "sinner's prayer" after she showed me the Roman verses. Here are a few of the verses:

> *"As it is written there is none righteous, no not one."*
> (Roman's 3:10)

> *"For all have sinned and fallen short of the glory of God."*
> (Roman's 3:23)

> *"But God demonstrated His own love toward us in that while we were yet sinners Christ died for us."*
> (Romans 5:8)

> *"Therefore, just as through one man sin entered into the world, and death through sin, and so death spread to all men, because all sinned."*
> (Romans 5:12)

> *"For the wages of sin is death, but the free gift of God is eternal life in Christ Jesus our Lord."*
> (Romans 6:23)

> *"That if you confess with your mouth Jesus as Lord, and believe in your heart that God raised Him from the dead, you shall be saved; for with the heart man believes, resulting in righteousness, and with the mouth confesses, resulting in salvation."*
> (Romans 10:9-10)

> *"For whoever will call upon the Name of the Lord will be saved."*
> (Romans 10:13)

> *"So faith comes from hearing, and hearing by the Word of Christ."*
> (Romans 10:17)

Paul led Onesimus to the Lord in Rome. By *"God-incidence,"* Onesimus was a slave of Philemon, whom Paul had also led to the Lord. The purpose of the letter is to appeal to Philemon with the sense of brotherhood to receive back the runaway slave, not as a slave, but as a brother in the Lord. The bottom line is, if Philemon did as Paul requested, the cause-and-effect in Paul would be refreshing.

> *"Yes, my brother, let me benefit from you in the Lord; refresh my heart in Christ."*
> (Philemon 1:20)

When we are in Christ, things don't just happen. God is on the move in our lives and in the lives of the people that we are interconnected.

> *"For perhaps he was for this reason parted from you for a while, that you should have him back forever."*
> (Philemon 1:15)

On the surface, it looked like a runaway slave, but in *"God-incidence"* it was for the purpose of restoration and refreshing.

PRAYER: Lord, help me see Your purposes in everything in life. Amen.

DAY 30
BLUES OF THE WILLOWS

"By the rivers of Babylon, there we sat down and wept, when we remembered Zion."

(Psalm 137:1)

The children of Israel were in a place of captivity and they were sitting down by the river weeping. The cause of weeping was remembrance of Zion where they were not. While they were in captivity, the captors were tormenting the captives by demanding that they sing some of their songs of Zion. In Psalm 137:4-6 we see that their response was:

- How can we sing the Lord's song in a foreign land?
- If I forget you, O Jerusalem may my right hand forget her skill (of plucking the harp).
- May my tongue cleave to the roof of my mouth.
- If I do not remember you.
- If I do not exalt Jerusalem above my chief joy.

Well, if that does not sound like the blues I don't know what does.

These types of psalms, or Psalms of Lament, are found throughout the Book of Psalms. This particular psalm is attributed to Jeremiah, who is also known as the Lamenter (for the book of Lamentations), the Weeping Prophet. In the Septuagint, it is attributed to him: "For David. By Jeremias, in the Captivity." (*translated from the Greek Septuagint by the Holy*

Transfiguration Monastery. (1974). The Psalter According to the Seventy. 1987, second printing. Boston MA: Holy Transfiguration Monastery. p. 241.

Most of the psalms like this sing the problem, and end with a declaration of how God is going to deliver them from their situations. However, this one takes a turn as the palmist expresses a prayer to seize and dash the little ones against the rock. (Psalm 137:9)

Some have tried to use this psalm as a reason *not* to sing songs and to hang up our guitars, and that would be right *if* we were captive. While we may be "strangers in a strange land" we are definitely not captive, because Jesus the Christ, the Anointed One, has broken our bondage and set us free.

> *"It was for freedom (not bondage) that Christ set us free…"*
> (Galatians 5:1, addition mine)

We have been delivered, transferred and redeemed and forgiven by "His Beloved Son."

> *"For He delivered us from the domain of darkness (by the rivers of Babylon captivity), and transferred (translated) us to the kingdom of His Beloved Son, in whom we have redemption, the forgiveness of sins."*
> (Colossians 1:13-14, addition mine)

We are *not* in captivity, but *"raised with Christ."*

> *"If then you have been raised up with Christ, keep seeking the things above, where Christ is seated at the right hand of God. Set your minds on the things above, not on the things that are on the earth, for you have died and your life is hidden with Christ in God."*
> (Colossians 3:1-3)

I understand the concept of the oppression of captivity and not singing the songs. At the same time, when we realized who we are and where we are in Him, it is hard not to sing and play. As a matter of fact, it is when we *do* sing and play those songs, it is then that the bonds become loosened and we walk in freedom, even in our captivity. As a matter of fact, if you look all around Psalm 137, you will see that it is surrounded with more verses to sing than not to sing.

So, get those harps down from the willow tree, tune them up, wake up that skillful right hand, and begin to sing those songs of going home.

PRAYER: Lord, thank You for setting me free in the midst of a lost and dying world. I will sing to let them know of my hope. Like John Fischer and Lord, "I am just one beggar telling another beggar where I found a loaf of bread." Amen.

DAY 31

THE INTEGRITY WALK

"Better is a poor man who walks in his integrity than he who is perverse in speech and is a fool."

(Pro-Verbs 19:1)

INTEGRITY: tom (tome)=From H8552; *completeness*; figuratively *prosperity*; usually (morally) *innocence*: - full, integrity, perfect (-ion), simplicity, upright (-ly, -ness), at a venture. **H8552: tamam (taw-mam')**=A primitive root; to *complete*, in a good or a bad sense, literally or figuratively, transitively or intransitively: - accomplish, cease, be clean [pass-] ed, consume, have done, (come to an, make an) end, fail, come to the full, be all gone, X be all here, be (make) perfect, be spent, sum, be (shew self) upright, be wasted, whole. (*Strong's*)

PERVERSE: 'iqqesh (ik-kashe')=From H6140; *distorted*; hence *false*: - crooked, froward, perverse. **H6140: 'aqash (aw-kash')**=A primitive root; to *knot* or *distort*; figuratively to *pervert* (act or declare perverse): - make crooked, (prove, that is) perverse (-rt). (*Strong's*)

Walking is a physical act of placing one foot in front of the other as you are going to a specific destination. Speech is the expression of thought that reveals the mind and determines your walk.

I equate integrity with character. The coach John Wooden is quoted as saying, "Character is how you act when no one is watching." The quality of your character, your integrity, or how you walk your life out before others is based on a conscience decision (aka choice).

In 1982, Edwin Louis Cole wrote a book called *Maximized Manhood*. On the back cover is a quote from the former cohost of *The 700 Club*, Ben Kinchlow: "Being a male is a matter of birth. Being a man is a matter of choice. This book is about that choice."

The choice that will change your perverse speech is to renew your mind with the Word of God. The saying that is peppered throughout this daily devotional reflects our thoughts, words, and actions.

> *"Unrestrained thoughts (what we think) produces unrestrained words (what we say) resulting in unrestrained actions (what we do)."*
>
> (Source Unknown)

When we begin to restrain what we think, the perverse speech will be changed into speech of integrity and the fool will become wise.

I have found over the years that my character and integrity is not a gift of the Spirit (1 Corinthians 12:1-10). It is fruit of the Spirit (Galatians 5:22-23) that is processed through pressure. In Romans 5:1-5, we see the process of character/integrity:

- Justified by faith
- Peace with God through our Lord Jesus Christ
- Obtained introduction by faith into the grace by which we stand
- Exult in hope of the glory of God
- Exult in our tribulations
- Tribulation brings about perseverance
- Perseverance brings about proven character/integrity
- Proven character brings about hope (confident expectation)

- Hope (confident expectation) does not disappoint
- The love of God is poured out within our hearts through the Holy Spirit.

PRAYER: Lord, thank You for the process of perfection (completion) and thank You that You can use the good, the bad, the ugly to bring about Your character and Your integrity in my life. Amen.

DAY 32
STRONGHOLD IN TROUBLED DAYS

"The Lord is good, a stronghold in the day of trouble, and He knows those who take refuge in Him."

(Nahum 1:7)

STRONGHOLD: ma'oz ma'uz ma'oz ma'uz (maw-oze', maw-ooz', maw-oze', maw-ooz')=From H5810; a *fortified* place; figuratively a *defence:* - force, fort (-ress), rock, strength (-en), (X most) strong (hold). **H5810: 'azaz** (aw-zaz')=A primitive root; to *be stout* (literally or figuratively): - harden, impudent, prevail, strengthen (self), be strong. (*Strong's*)

TROUBLE: tsarah (tsaw-raw')= *tightness* (that is, figuratively *trouble*); transitively a female *rival:* - adversary, adversity, affliction, anguish, distress, tribulation, trouble. (*Strong's*)

As I look around, it appears that we not only have *a day* (single) *of trouble* but we have *many days* (plural) *of troubles*. A cursory perusal of radio, television, newspapers, internet, and just life around us, shows that we are in need of a stronghold.

I like the first part of the definition of trouble where it says, *tightness*. In the movie, *O Brother Where Art Thou*, the three main characters were surrounded by the police. The character played by George Clooney describes the trouble they are in, "…we're in a tight spot!" They needed a strong tower because the barn that they were hiding in was being burned.

> *"The name of the LORD is a strong tower; the righteous runs into it and is safe."*
>
> (Pro-Verbs 18:10)

In the passage from Nahum, it is the second time God is dealing with Nineveh. The first time God used Jonah to pronounce the message of judgement and their need to repent. They repented; God relented; Jonah got angry and suicidal because they repented and God did not bring the hammer down on them. In the book of Nahum, it is one hundred years later and Nineveh is once again on the forefront with the need to repent. This time there will be a different outcome; fifty years later, they will be utterly destroyed. I think that the companion verse with Nahum is Galatians 6:7-9.

> *"Do not be deceived, God is not mocked; for whatever a man sows, this he will also reap. For the one who sows to his own flesh shall from the flesh reap corruption, but the one who sows to the Spirit that from the Spirit reaps eternal life."*
>
> (Galatians 6:7-8)

Here are a few things that stand out in Nahum 1:7:

- The Lord is good: He is not bad. His heartbeat is good and He desires good things for His people.
- There is a day of trouble: This is a day that is filled with tightness, adversity with an adversary, afflictions, anguish, distress, and tribulation.
- This good Lord is a stronghold in the day of trouble.
- In the middle of trouble, as people run into the stronghold (the name of the Lord), the Lord knows who takes refuge in Him.

That last one is a comfort, "the Lord who knows who takes refuge in Him." What happens if Nineveh does not take refuge, or for that matter, what happens if we do not take refuge in the strong tower, the Name of the Lord, Jesus, God is Salvation?

> *"But with an overflowing flood He will make a complete end of its site, and will pursue His enemies into the darkness."*
> (Nahum 1:8)

Fifty years later, Nahum 1:8 took place as He made, *"a complete end of its site…"*

PRAYER: Lord, thank You for Your name—God is Salvation, the Strong Tower—and thank You for saving me. Amen.

DAY 33
CONFIDENTLY ENTER THIS WAY

"Since therefore brethren we have confidence to enter the holy place by the blood of Jesus."

(Hebrews 10:19)

CONFIDENCE/BOLDNESS: parrhesia (par-rhay-see'-ah)=*all out spokenness*, that is, *frankness, bluntness, publicity*; by implication *assurance:* - bold (X -ly, -ness, -ness of speech), confidence, X freely, X openly, X plainly (-ness). (*Strong's*)

The Holy Place was a place in the Temple that was holy. Now that seems simple enough to understand. Another obvious thought is that something unholy does not need to be entering into a holy place.

If you have a glass of water that is pure and pristine, you have confidence to drink that glass of water to quench your thirst. But if you put in a tablespoon of poison, you may not be as confident to drink the water. Why? Because the pure, pristine, refreshing glass of water, (let's call that the holy place) was adulterated by the entrance of the poison, (let's call that the unholy), which in turn will affect whoever would drink the water. All confidence is gone.

In the Old Testament, God ordered the construction of the Tabernacle. It was broken down into three areas: (1) the outer court, (2) the inner court, (3) the innermost court.

The outer court was used to bring the sacrifices for the people's sins to be slaughtered and burnt along with a laver for washing. The inner court was a place of preparation for the High Priest prior to entering the Holy of Holies or the innermost court. The Holy of Holies was the dwelling place of God where His presence would rest on the Mercy Seat and sacrifices were received. After the Tabernacle in the wilderness, there would eventually be a stone edifice in Jerusalem called the Temple, with the same type of set up of sacrifices, offerings, forgiveness and worship. Only the priests were allowed to go into the Holy Place.

With Jesus being crucified on the cross in our place as the "propitiation," the satisfactory substitute for our sins—and the burial and the resurrection from the dead on the third day—things shifted from perpetual animal offerings and one person going into the presence of God, to Jesus being the final and ultimate sacrifice and our access into God's presence. From where does this confidence come?

- By the blood of Jesus
- It is a new and living way
- He inaugurated it for us
- It is through the veil, that is His flesh

As Jesus hung on the cross as the satisfactory substitute for our sins (propitiation), He breathed His last breath and commended His spirit back to the Father, the cause-and-effect in the world that He left behind was chaotic. Darkness, earthquakes, split rocks, resurrection of dead bodies coming out of the tombs that were seen by many people. (See Matthew 27:50-66 for details.)

Activity took place in the Temple that will be referred to in the book of Hebrews a few years later.

> *"And behold, the veil of the temple was torn in two from top to bottom..."*
>
> (Matthew 27:51a; Mark 15:38)

> *"...to enter the holy place by the blood of Jesus, by a new and living way which He inaugurated for us through the veil, that is His flesh."*
>
> (Hebrews 10:19-20)

Historically, the veil was torn in two from top to bottom. Theologians suggest this represents that this heavy veil was not torn by man's decision, but by God's decision as it came from the top to bottom and not from bottom to top.

Jesus's flesh was considered to be the veil that was ripped. His blood flowed from the ripped veil, which made now holy whoever passed through the veil into the presence of God. That person could step into His presence with confidence and not hold back because of sin. The idea of confidence is not arrogance, but humble confidence entering into the presence of God Almighty with fear and trembling.

PRAYER: Lord, thank You for this new and living way (Jesus is alive) by which I have access to Your presence, to Your mercy, to Your love. Amen.

DAY 34

THE DIRECTED WILL

"I will..."

(Psalm 138:1-2)

Whenever I hear the phrase, "I will," it makes me think that someone has made a choice, a conscious decision to do something. They are exercising their volition, their free will to carry out a certain act. I understand that they are not being forced to do a certain thing, but really want to do whatever that they are willing themselves to do.

The psalmist, who was also a king, states that he will do three things and the recipient of his will and choice is the Great *Thee and Thy*...a.k.a. God, the Lord, the Creator of the Universe, the King of Kings and the Lord of Lords. The psalmist states that He will:

- Give Thee thanks

THANKS: yadah (yaw-daw')=A primitive root; used only as denominative from H3027; literally to *use* (that is, hold out) *the hand*; physically to *throw* (a stone, an arrow) at or away; especially to *revere* or *worship* (with extended hands); intensively to *bemoan* (by wringing the hands): - cast (out), (make) confess (-ion), praise, shoot, (give) thank (-ful, -s, -sgiving). (*Strong's*)

- Sing praises to Thee

PRAISE: zawmar (zaw-mar'**)**=A primitive root (perhaps identical with H2168 through the idea of *striking* with the fingers); properly to *touch* the strings or parts of a musical instrument, that is, *play* upon it; to make *music*, accompanied by the voice; hence to *celebrate* in song and music: - give praise, sing forth praises, psalms. (*Strong's*)

- Give thanks to Thy name.

WORSHIP: shawkaw (shaw-khaw**)'**=A primitive root; to *depress*, that is, *prostrate* (especially reflexively in homage to royalty or God): - bow (self) down, crouch, fall down (flat), humbly beseech, do (make) obeisance, do reverence, make to stoop, worship. (*Strong's*)

I believe that if we choose to do those three things, our lives will be a lot less complicated. When our will lines up with His will, we begin to think more clearly, hear His voice more distinctly, and begin to move and walk with confidence that we are on the right road in life.

When you choose to give thanks, sing praises, and bow down and worship Him, be sure to do it like the psalmist who:

- Gives thanks *with all my heart*
- Sing praises to Him *before the gods (don't be ashamed)*
- Bow down towards His holy temple and, while bowing, give thanks for the reason you can do it: His lovingkindness (mercy) and His truth (His Word is truth).

PRAYER: Lord, thank You for my free will. I choose to use that free will to worship You today. Amen.

DAY 35
BACK TO THE DRAWING OUT BOARD

"A plan in the heart of a man is like deep water, but a man of understanding draws it out."
(Pro-Verbs 20:5)

"The best laid schemes o' mice an' men / Gang aft a-gley"
(*To A Mouse* by Robert Burns)

"The best-laid plans of mice and men often go awry."
(English translation of *To a Mouse*)

"No matter how carefully a project is planned, something may still go wrong with it."

(Dictionary.com)

Plans are formatted in the brain, in our thoughts, as we devise how we should do certain things. There is a big difference where we formulate plans in our human thinking and when God plants a desire in our hearts. When I come up with something, it is usually superficial; but when God gives me a plan, it is planted deep within me.

DEEP: amoq (aw-moke')=From H6009; *deep* (literally or figuratively): - (X exceeding) deep (thing) **H6009: amaq** (aw-mak') =A primitive root; to *be* (causatively *make*) *deep* (literally or figuratively): - (be, have, make, seek) deep (-ly), depth, be profound. (*Strong's*)

"Delight yourself in the Lord and He will give you (plant within you) the desires of your heart."
(Psalm 37:4, addition mine)

DELIGHT: Anag (aw-nag)=A primitive root; to be *soft* or pliable, that is, (figuratively) *effeminate* or luxurious: - delicate (-ness), (have) delight (self), sport self. (*Strong's*)

Drawing out God's plans for us takes an ability to be soft and pliable to Him. To be able to yield our will to Him is where we come into an understanding of His plans for us.

UNDERSTANDING: tabun tebunah tobunah (taw-boon', teb-oo-naw', to-boo-naw')= *intelligence*; by implication an *argument*; by extension *caprice:* - discretion, reason, skilfulness, understanding, wisdom. (*Strong's*)

Once you come into an understanding of those deep water plans that God has planted, then you may be able to implement those plans under the guidance of the Great Plan Maker: God Himself. The thing is to be able to not make your own plans without submission to the Lord. Don't just arbitrarily announce what you will, or will not, do. The key is to make sure your plans line up with God's plan, His will for your life.

"Come now you who say, 'today or tomorrow, we shall go to such and such a city, and spend a year there and engage in business and make a profit.' Yet you do not know what your life will be like tomorrow. You are just a vapor that appears for a little while and then vanishes away. Instead, you ought to say, 'If the Lord wills, we shall live and also do this or that.'"
James 4:13-15, emphasis mine)

PRAYER: Lord, I lay my plans on the altar and cry out, "If You will." Amen.

DAY 36

THE YET FACTOR

"Yet I will exult in the Lord, I will rejoice in the God of my salvation."

(Habakkuk 3:18)

Habakkuk questions and prophesied about Judah, and judgment as wickedness is on a rampage. Historically, King Josiah was considered a good king. After Josiah's death, all the good that he has instituted was dismantled by a series of bad kings. This opens the door to evil and bad men.

The question is why is God not coming to the rescue of His covenant people? The answer is that God is using the Babylonians (Chaldeans) to mete out His justice and punishment. As usual, we see God's covenant people reaping what they sowed, but we also see God in His redemptive nature.

Between the point of punishment and the point of redemption, there is a time frame where we do not see appear to see God doing anything. Isn't that how it is in our lives?

In the Sunday school class that I teach (The Ruminator's Sunday School Class) we often talk about the place between prayer and provision and we call it "the land called nitty-gritty." This is the land where we *"walk by faith and not by sight"* and not by things *"revealed to our senses"* (2 Corinthians 5:7; Hebrews 11:1, The Amplified Bible).

> *"Behold, as for the proud ones (Babylonians/Chaldeans) his soul is not right within him; but the righteous (the covenant people) shall live by faith."*
>
> (Habakkuk 2:4, addition mine)

This phrase is used three other times in the New Testament. (Romans 1:17, Galatians 3:11, Hebrews 10:38). Habakkuk lays out the things that they may see in Habakkuk 3:17:

- The fig tree should not blossom
- No fruit on the vines
- Fields produce no food
- Flock cut off from the field
- No cattle in the stalls

This is the reality of their situation. Imagine what your situation is like.

- There is no sign of prosperity.
- There is no harvest from your hard work.
- There is no money in your bank account.
- Things seem to be cut off from reaching you.
- There is nothing in your 401K.

When you walk by faith and not by sight…you have to institute *the yet factor*. That is where reality screams at you, *yet* you choose not to worry or fret or be anxious about reality, but choose to act differently.

- Yet I will exult in the Lord.
- Yet I will rejoice in the God of my salvation.
- Yet I will declare that the Lord God is my strength.
- The Lord has made my feet like hinds' feet.
- The Lord makes me walk on my high places

The bottom line is that the Lord is in control no matter what it looks like; no matter what it feels like; no matter I see or don't see. *Yet* (in spite of what I see) *I will* (my choice and conscious decision by my free will choose) think, speak, and do differently.

PRAYER: Thank you Lord for options of choice. *Yet I will choose You, Lord.* Amen.

DAY 37
ANTI-QUARRELS AND ANTI-CONFLICTS

"What is the source of quarrels and conflicts among you?"
(James 4:1)

As of this writing, the world is filled with quarrels and conflicts and continues to get worse. All around the world, there are people trying to resolve issues on a global scale and individuals continue to struggle on a personal level.

The problem is that no one is striking at the root of the quarrels and conflicts. They deal with the surface but with time, the same problems return as strong as ever. Like a weed that will continue to grow and cause problems unless the root of the weed is killed and pulled, so it is with quarrels and conflicts among you. James identifies the cause right of the bat.

"Is not the source your pleasures that wage war in your members?"
(James 4:1)

PLEASURES/LUSTS: hedone (hay-don-ay')=From ανδάνω handanō (to *please*); sensual *delight*; by implication *desire:* - lust, pleasure. (*Strong's*)

LUST: epithumeo (ep-ee-thoo-meh'-o)= to set the *heart upon*, that is, *long* for (rightfully or otherwise): - covet, desire, would fain, lust (after). (*Strong's*)

The first definition speaks of the plurality of the actual things, while the second definition speaks of the acts of *going* after the things. When we set our hearts and long for those things that please ourselves other than pleasing God, we enter into quarrels and conflicts that start within our own being and manifest outwardly towards others. We want what they've got.

Let's look at an overview of the problem and then we will look at the solution.

- You lust and do not have, so you commit murder.
- You are envious and cannot obtain, so you fight and quarrel.
- You do not have because you do not ask.
- You ask and do not receive, because you ask with wrong motives so you that you may spend it on your pleasures.
- You don't realize that friendship with the world is hostility towards God.
- When you make yourself a friend with the world, that makes you an enemy with God.

We were created not for quarreling and conflicts, but created for the Spirit to dwell within us and this is all based on His grace. All of these things listed are our choice and our will to follow His choices and will for us.

- He gives a greater grace.
- God is opposed to the proud but gives grace to the humble
- Submit to God.
- Resist the d-evil and he will flee from you.
- Draw near to God, He will draw near to you.
- Cleanse your hands.
- Purify your hearts.
- Humble yourself in the presence of the Lord.
- Get ready to be exalted.
- Do not speak against one another.

- Do not judge your brother.
- Do not speak against the law.
- Do not judge the law.

PRAYER: Lord, please help me to yield my lusts to Your grace. Amen.

DAY 38

THE HOUND OF HEAVEN: WHERE CAN I GO

"Where can I go from Thy Spirit or where can I flee from Thy presence?"

(Psalm 139:7)

SPIRIT: ruach (roo'-akh**)**=From H7306; *wind*; by resemblance *breath*, that is, a sensible (or even violent) exhalation; figuratively *life, anger, unsubstantiality*; by extension a *region* of the sky; by resemblance *spirit*, but only of a rational being (including its expression and functions): - air, anger, blast, breath, X cool, courage, mind, X quarter, X side, spirit ([-ual]), tempest, X vain, ([whirl-]) wind (-y). **H7306: ruach (**roo'-akh**)**=A primitive root; properly to *blow*, that is, *breathe*; only (literally) to *smell* or (by implication *perceive* (figuratively to *anticipate, enjoy*): - accept, smell, X touch, make of quick understanding. (*Strong's*)

PRESENCE: panıym (paw-neem'**)**=the *face* (as the part that *turns*) (*Strong's*)

When God formed man from a lump of clay and breathed His breath into His nostrils, God came Face (His presence) to face (Adam/man) and His Spirit jumpstarted the lump of clay into a living soul. (Genesis 2:7) When man/woman sinned (disobedience in the Garden) God came looking for man, but the man and wo-man hid themselves from His presence. (Genesis 3:8-9) Ever since then mankind has run from the Presence and the Spirit of God. In the words of the Temptation's song *Ball of Confusion,* even though we may run, we can never hide.

Psalm 139 is a psalm declaring God's Omnipresence and Omniscience in connection with His creation.

Omnipresence: present everywhere at the same time

Omniscience: having complete or unlimited knowledge, awareness, or understanding; perceiving all things

- Thou hast searched me and known me.
- Thou dost know when I sit down and when I rise up.
- Thou dost understand thought from afar.
- Thou dost scrutinize my path and my lying down.
- Thou art intimately acquainted with all my ways
- Even before there is a word on my tongue, Thou dost know it all.
- Thou hast enclosed me behind and before.
- Thou hast laid Thy hand upon me.

Knowing all that He knows about me fills me with wonder, which makes it wonderful (full of wonder). This is like the top shelf where I can't reach it. That is the level of how my mind can fathom how well You know me.

Where can I go from Your Spirit and where can I flee from Your presence? Of course, the answer is nowhere. I think about Jonah who tried to run from Your presence. Even to the depths of the ocean in the belly of a great fish, he could not escape.

The next question that comes to mind is, "Why in the world would I want to escape your presence?" I know that, according to Acts 3:19, that there is, *"refreshing in your presence."* Let's check out to the psalmist and check out potential hiding places.

- Ascend to heaven
- Make my bed in Sheol (nether world)
- Take wings of the dawn
- Dwell in the remotest part of the sea
- In the darkness it is not dark
- In the night it is bright as day
- Darkness and light are alike to You.

Even before I was born You were there.

- Thou didst form my inward parts.
- Thou didst weave me in my mother's womb.
- I am fearfully and wonderfully made.
- I am one of Your words and I am wonderful because You made me.
- My soul knows it all so well.
- My frame is not hidden from Thee.
- I was made in secret and skillfully wrought in the depths of the earth.
- Your eyes have seen my unformed substance.
- I was ordained and written in the book when as yet there was not one of them.

Well, apparently you can't run or hide or get away from God. In the same vein, nothing can separate us from the love of God.

> *"Who shall separate us from the love of Christ? Shall tribulation, or distress, or persecution, or famine, or nakedness, or peril, or sword?"*
>
> (Romans 8:35)

> *"But in all these things we overwhelmingly conquer through Him who loved us. For I am convinced that neither death, nor life, nor angels, nor principalities, nor things present, nor things to*

come, nor powers, nor height, nor depth, no any other created thing, shall be able to separate us from the love of God, which is in Christ."

(Romans 8:37-39)

PRAYER: Lord, thank You that there is nowhere that I can run that You can't find me, and once You find me, there is nothing that can separate me from Your love. Amen.

DAY 39

THE WANDERING MAN

"A man who wanders from the way of understanding will rest in the assembly of the dead."

(Pro-Verbs 21:16)

WANDERS: ta'ah (taw-aw')=A primitive root; to *vacillate*, that is, *reel* or *stray* (literally or figuratively); also causatively of both: - (cause to) go astray, deceive, dissemble, (cause to, make to) err, pant, seduce, (make to) stagger, (cause to) wander, be out of the way. (*Strong's*)

The place that you want to move towards is the *way of understanding*. How sad it is to see someone reeling, staggering, and wandering away from a place of understanding into a gathering place of dead wanderers. The man that wanders away thinks that they are moving in the correct direction.

"Every man's way is right in his own eyes, but the Lord weighs the heart."

(Pro-Verbs 21:2)

"There is a way which seemeth right unto a man, but the end thereof are the ways of death."

(Pro-Verbs 14:12, KJV)

In our passage, the man does three things which will have a negative effect in his life.

- The man who wanders from the way of understanding.
- The man who loves pleasure.
- The man who loves wine and oil.

The cause-and-effects are:

- Wanders: Rests in the assembly of the dead
- Loves pleasure: Will become a poor man
- Loves wine and oil: Will not become rich

I shake my head as I read about this man, wondering, *"How stupid can a man be?"* But, as usually is the case, when I feel superior to people I read about in the Bible—and even people I know—the Lord will allow me to see that *I am that man*. I am the man who, in my mind, knows a better way to go and ends up wandering from the Lord's wisdom. I am the man who loves pleasurable things in my life and will do anything I can to ensure that I have those things. I am the man who loves the comfort of wine and oil as I numb myself to the pains of this life.

PRAYER: Lord, forgive me for wandering away from Your understanding towards temporary pleasures and comfort. Amen.

DAY 40
THE HIDDEN SEEKER

"Seek the Lord, all you humble of the earth who have carried out His ordinances; seek righteousness, seek humility. Perhaps you will be hidden in the day of the Lord's anger."

(Zephaniah 2:3)

SEEK: baqash (baw-kash')=A primitive root; to *search* out (by any method; specifically in worship or prayer); by implication to *strive after*: - ask, beg, beseech, desire, enquire, get, make inquisition, procure, (make) request, require, seek (for). (*Strong's*)

The prophet Zephaniah is proclaiming the judgment of God on Judah and eventually the Gentile nations. Why? He is speaking because of their sins and that God will judge. There is also a warning of *the great day of the Lord.*

Of course, with God's proclamation of judgment, He always extends restoration if they turn to Him. In the midst of the nation there are people who are not sinning, who are humble people, who carry out his ordinances, and seek His righteousness. The word of hope to them is that, *"perhaps you will be hidden in the day of the Lord's anger."* (Zephaniah 2:3) I don't know about you but I want the *"perhaps of the Lord"* in my life. I like them odds.

It appears that the key to *"perhaps"* being *"hidden in the day of the Lord's anger"* is to someone who searches out and strives after the Lord and not sin. To seek the Lord means to humbly seek righteousness and humility. This make perfect sense as you read in 1 Peter 5 that:

> *"God is opposed to the proud, but gives grace to the humble. Humble yourselves, therefore, under the mighty hand of God that He may exalt you at the proper time, casting all your anxiety upon Him, because He cares for you."*
> (1 Peter 5:5-7)

Instead of seeking my way or seeking sin or anything that displeases God, my seeking is the Lord Himself. When Jesus taught His disciples how to pray, one aspect was to pray:

"Thy Kingdom come, Thy will be done on earth as it is in heaven."

(Matthew 6:10)

That means that we *seek the Lord's will* on Earth where we live and breathe.

The Lord's will is that you seek Him and find Him. The Lord is not playing a game of *hide and seek*, where you do your part in seeking Him and then—at the end of the game—He does not allow you to find Him. On a human level, when we hide eggs for our kid's Easter Egg Hunt, we do not hide the eggs so that they will never find the eggs. No, we place them where they can be found.

> *"But from there you will seek the Lord your God, and you will find Him if you search for Him with all your heart."*
> (Deuteronomy 4:29)

My problem is when I seek and search for Him but I don't do it with all my heart. I search for Him half-heartedly, maybe out of fear that I might find Him and will be confronted with my sin and my need for Him.

Between Genesis and Revelation, there are 244 mentions of the word *seek*. You kind of get the idea that we are to be not only *believers* but also *seekers*.

Jesus told His followers to be seekers. In Matthew He speaks of the tenacity of seeking His kingdom and His righteousness. The Amplified Bible brings out the tenacious aspect of seeking.

> *"Keep on asking and it will be given you; keep on seeking and you will find; keep on knocking (reverently) and the door will be opened to you. For everyone who keeps on asking receives, and he who keeps on seeking finds, and to him who keeps on knocking it will be opened."*
> (Matthew 7:7-8/The Amplified Bible)

I find that when I am not receiving, when I am not finding, and when the doors of Heaven appear to be closed, that is not the time to stop; but the time to keep on keeping on. When I am seeking the Lord and righteousness and humility, sometimes you keep on by faith with expectancy to be *hidden in the day of His anger.*

PRAYER: Lord, I am keeping on keeping on until You return, to seek Your face of approval. I pray that You will find faith on Earth and a bunch of seekers, including me. Amen.

DAY 41
THE PURPOSE OF INHERITANCE

"...for you were called for the very purpose that you might inherit a blessing."

(1 Peter 3:9)

INHERIT: kleronomeo (klay-ron-om-eh'-o)=From G2818; to *be an heir* to (literally or figuratively): - be heir, (obtain by) inherit (-ance). **G2818: kleronomos** (klay-ron-om'-os)= (in its original sense of *partitioning*, that is, [reflexively] *getting* by apportionment); a *sharer by lot*, that is, an *inheritor* (literally or figuratively); by implication a *possessor*: - heir. (*Strong's*)

BLESSING: Eulogia (yoo-log-ee'-ah)= *fine speaking*, that is, *elegance of language*; *commendation* ("eulogy"), that is, (reverentially) *adoration*; religiously, *benediction*; by implication *consecration*; by extension *benefit* or *largess*: - blessing (a matter of) bounty (X -tifully), fair speech. (*Strong's*)

Sometimes a follower of Jesus looks for their *calling* or their *purpose*. What we don't realize is that we already have a calling and purpose that we are supposed to walk in until He returns. Here are a few examples of calling and purpose.

- *Follow Me* (Matthew 4:19): Originally given out to some fishermen but expanded to us via *The Great Commission* found in Matthew 28:19-20, where Jesus told His original called ones to go and make disciples, baptize them, and then teach the disciples to *observe all that He commanded them.* When Jesus was praying for His followers to be sanctified in truth (the Word), He said that He was not just praying for those original ones who answered the call to follow Him, but also for those who believed in Him (you and me) through their (their witness) Word.

- *Called according to His purpose* (Romans 8:28): Whatever happens in our lives (good, bad, or ugly) we can rest assured that He will cause all thing to work together for certain people. These are the ones who: (1) love God (2) the called (3) according to His purpose. The calling was to be predestined to be conformed to the image of His Son so Jesus would be the first born of many brethren.
- *Called for this purpose* (1 Peter 2:21): To suffer without complaining. To endure hardship even when you are doing the right thing. This finds favor with God. In this calling and example, Jesus set the example for us to follow in His steps: (1) He committed no sin (2) no deceit found in His mouth (3) when reviled, He did not revile in return (4) while suffering, He uttered no threats (4) He kept entrusting Himself to Him who judges righteously.

We live a life that is meant to inherit a blessing versus a curse. The flow of thought to inherit this blessing is to watch your mouth and act accordingly. As you read the second and third chapters of 1 Peter, you see it is about our relationship to all people—good, bad, and ugly—and how we react towards those who do us wrong, will determine who we are trusting; humans or God. In 1 Peter 3:8-9, Peter sums up what he is talking about:

- Let/Allow all be harmonious
- Let/Allow all be sympathetic
- Let/Allow all be brotherly
- Let/Allow all be kindhearted

- Let/Allow all be humble in spirit
- Don't return evil for evil
- Don't return insult for insult
- Give a blessing instead

Why do these things? Because you were called for the very purpose of inheriting a blessing, and when you do not give a blessing because of poor attitude, you negate your blessing.

PRAYER: Father, help me to follow Your example, to walk in Your footstep, to trust You when people treat me badly. Thank You for Your called blessing. I will bless others. Amen.

DAY 42
NAME THANKERS AND PRESENCE DWELLERS

"Surely the righteous will give thanks to Thy name; the upright will dwell in Thy presence."

(Psalm 140:13)

Once again, the psalmist sings for protection against the wicked. The wicked are characterized as:

- Evil men
- Violent men
- Devisors of evil
- Stirrers of war
- Sharp serpent/viper like tongues with poison under their lips
- Wicked hands
- Men of violence
- Ones with lips of mischief

The psalmist asks God for four things:

- Rescue me from evil men.
- Preserve me from violent men.
- Keep me from hands of the wicked.
- Preserve me from violent men who have purposed to trip up my feet.

The psalmist then makes a wonderful declaration that he wants us to ponder as he interjects in the middle of the psalm: *Selah*.

SELAH: selah (seh'-law**)**=From H5541; *suspension* (of music), that is, *pause:* - Selah. **H5541: salah (**saw-law'**)**=A primitive root; to *hang* up, that is, *weigh*, or (figuratively) *contemn:* - tread down (under foot), value. (*Strong's*)

> *"I said to the Lord, 'Thou art my God; Give ear, O Lord, to the voice of my supplications. O God the Lord, the strength of my salvation, Thou hast covered my head in the day of battle. Do not grant, O Lord, the desires of the wicked; Do not promote his evil device, lest they be exalted. [Selah]'"*
> (Psalm 140:6-8)

This passage brings the psalmist's passionate prayers against the evil and violent men. The bottom line for the righteous is underscored in the last verse.

> *"Surely the righteous will give thanks to Thy name; the upright will dwell in Thy presence."*
> (Psalm 140:13)

PRAYER: Lord, thank You for Your presence where I can dwell in a world full of evil. Amen.

DAY 43
READY LIPS

"For it will be pleasant if you keep them within you, that they may be ready on your lips."

(Pro-Verbs 22:18)

For your lips to be ready to speak words of wisdom and words of knowledge, you must do four things first.

- Incline your ears.
- Hear the words of the wise.
- Apply you mind to knowledge.
- Keep them (wise words and knowledge) within you.

Why do you want to actively do these things on purpose? So you can keep and speak these wise and knowledgeable words on your lips. Why do you need these wise and knowledgeable words on your lips?

"So that your trust may be in the Lord, I have taught you today, even you."

(Pro-Verbs 22:19)

TRUST: mibtach (mib-tawkh')=From H982; properly a *refuge*, that is, (objectively) *security*, or (subjectively) *assurance:* - confidence, hope, sure, trust. **H982: batach** (baw-takh')=A primitive root; properly to *hie* for refuge (but not so *precipitately* as H2620); figuratively to *trust*, be *confident* or *sure:* - be bold (confident, secure, sure), careless (one, woman), put confidence, (make to) hope, (put, make to) trust. (*Strong's*)

Why do we need to have this kind of wisdom and knowledge on our lips so that *our trust may be in the Lord*? Well, everyone out in the world is not for you. Everyone out in the world does not trust in the Lord. Who are these people? In Pro-Verbs 22:8-16, we see the cast of characters:

- The borrower
- The sower/reaper of iniquity
- Scoffers
- Strife and dishonor
- The treacherous man
- The sluggard man
- The adulterous woman
- Foolish child
- Oppressor of the poor

To discern those types of people, you need to incline your ear, you need to hear the words of the wise. You need to go beyond inclining and hearing but also apply your mind to this knowledge. It is like faith without works, or corresponding actions, is dead (James 2:17); so it is with wisdom and knowledge not utilized.

PRAYER: Lord, thank You for wisdom that I can use in a practical way. I will apply what I hear speak to my inclined ear. My lips are ready to speak Your wisdom. Amen.

DAY 44
CONSIDER YOUR WAYS...AGAIN

"Thus says the Lord of hosts, 'Consider your ways!'"

(Haggai 1:7)

Haggai is a book about rebuilding the Temple. The Jewish people had been in exile for 70 years and had come out ready to listen, and Haggai was speaking. Haggai was speaking about restoration of the Temple, building the house of the Lord. They were encouraged to *"Consider your ways."* (Haggai 1:5; Haggai 1:7)

CONSIDER: lebab (lay-bawb')=From H3823; the *heart* (as the most interior organ); used also like H3820: - + bethink themselves, breast, comfortably, courage, ([faint], [tender-] heart([-ed]), midst, mind, X unawares, understanding. **H3823: labab** (law-bab')=A primitive root; properly to *be enclosed* (as if with *fat*); by implication (as denominative from H3824) to *unheart*, that is, (in a good sense) *transport* (with love), or (in a bad sense) *stultify*; also (as denominative from H3834) to *make cakes:* - make cakes, ravish, be wise. (*Strong's*)

WAYS: Derek (deh'-rek)=From H1869; a *road* (as *trodden*); figuratively a *course* of life or *mode* of action, often adverbially: - along, away, because of, + by, conversation, custom, [east-] ward, journey, manner, passenger, through, toward, [high-] [path-] way [-side], whither [-soever]. **H1869: darak** (daw-rak')=A primitive root; to *tread*; by implication to *walk*; also to *string* a bow (by treading on it in bending): - archer, bend, come, draw, go (over), guide, lead (forth), thresh, tread (down), walk. (*Strong's*)

The ways that they were considering were about the cause-and-effect of their previous rebellion.

The cause-and-effect of their rebellion is reflected in Haggai 1:6, 9-11.

- Sown much but harvested little
- Eat but there is not enough to be satisfied
- Drink but there is not enough to get drunk
- Put on clothing but no one is warm enough
- Earn wages to put in a purse with holes
- Look for much but it comes to little
- Bring it home and He blows it away
- The sky withholds its dew
- The earth has withheld its produce
- A drought is called on the land, mountains, grains, new wine, oil, ground produce, men, cattle, and on all the labors of your hands.

Two things took place as Zerubbabel, Joshua (not son of Nun) the High Priest and all the remnant of the people did two things. They: (1) obeyed the voice of the Lord (2) showed reverence for the Lord. The cause-and-effect of them doing these things was what we all want in our lives.

> "*Then Haggai, the messenger of the Lord, spoke by the commission of the Lord to the people, 'I am with you, declares the Lord.'*"
>
> (Haggai 1:13)

It is amazing what will take place when we consider our ways. The stirring of the Lord begins to move and we begin to come and work. They came and worked on the house. (Haggai 1:14)

There is another place where that word *"consider"* is used that will also affect us if we will consider.

> *"Therefore, holy brethren, partakers of a heavenly calling,* consider Jesus, *the Apostle and High Priest of our confession."*
> (Hebrews 3:1, emphasis mine)

The context of this verse is how faithful Jesus was to the Father Who had appointed Jesus as the One who established us and administered the sacrifice where we could come into His (The Father's) presence. The writer of Hebrews begins to speak of a building, and how that building of every house was built by someone, but the builder of all things is God. As faithful as Moses was, there was Someone even more faithful over His house.

> *"But Christ was faithful as a Son over His house Whose house we are, if we hold fast our confidence and the boast of our hope firm until the end."*
> (Hebrews 3:6)

PRAYER: I am considering my way, which happens to be You. You are my way, my truth, my life, and I come to the Father through You. Amen.

DAY 45
THE RETURN OF THE TRUE PRO-VERB

"It has happened to them according to the true pro-verb, a dog returns to its own vomit, and a sow, after washing, returns to wallowing in the mire."
(2 Peter 2:22; Pro-Verbs 26:11, addition mine)

TRUE: alethes (al-ay-thace'**)**= *true (as not concealing)*: - true, truly, truth. (*Strong's*)

PROVERB: Paroimia (par-oy-mee'-ah**)**= a state *alongside of supposition*, that is, (concretely) an *adage*; specifically an enigmatical or fictitious *illustration:* - parable, proverb. (*Strong's*)

A pro-verb is something used to illustrate truth. This is accomplished by not concealing the truth, but rather revealing the truth. Peter gleans from the book of Pro-Verbs (the book of positive action) by comparing false teachers and people who follow those false teachers to dogs and pigs. It is good advice for people who return to their pre-Christ days as they exchange the truth for a lie. I personally have experience with dogs and pigs as I returned to my old lifestyle. Some call it backsliding, but I call it sliding face forward into the muck and the mire that I was delivered from in the first place.

You might have seen a dog eating to the point of throwing up (vomiting) and eating the vomit; if you are like me, you are gagging. If you have ever seen a pig cleaned and then immediately go back to the slop and wallow around and become just as filthy as if it had not been clean in the first place. Again, this is a perfect picture of me getting saved in 1970, and by 1972, I returned to the vomit and mire by smoking more dope, sniffing more chemicals, drinking more booze, and then doing more stupid stuff than I did before I was saved.

This pro-verb truly illustrated my sin that was no longer concealed. It revealed the cause-and-effect and the sowing and reaping of living in the flesh and not living in the Spirit.

Returning to the vomit and mire would have be a sad state of affair if that was the only returning I did. I made a major decision with another return.

RETURN: epistrepho☐ (ep-ee-stref'-o)= to *revert* (literally, figuratively or morally): - come (go) again, convert, (re-) turn (about, again). (*Strong's*)

After a little over a year of eating vomit and rolling around in the mucky mire, I did like the prodigal son who was eating with the pigs. I came to my senses and figured out that what I had left to satisfy the lusts of my flesh, eyes, and the boastful pride of life was not very fulfilling.

I returned by a choice called *repentance*. I hungered and desired to be refreshed again and not drained, malnourished, and dehydrated. I choose to repent and return.

> "Repent *therefore and* return, *that your sins may be wiped away, in order that times of* refreshing *may come from the presence of the Lord."*
>
> (Acts 3:19, emphasis mine)

REPENT: metanoeo (met-an-o-eh'-o)= to *think differently* or *afterwards*, that is, *reconsider* (morally to *feel compunction*): - repent. (*Strong's*)

I found that I could repent. If I don't return, I merely have remorse that I got caught in my sins; the truth was no longer concealed about me; and I am experiencing cause-and-effect of my sins. I must have a change of heart, a change of mind, a change of direction by turning around and return to the Lord.

Peter used his letter to stir up the believers' sincere minds. He reminded them that they should remember the words spoken before by the holy prophets and the commandment of the Lord and Savior spoken by the apostles. (2 Peter 3:1-2)

PRAYER: Lord, thank You that I don't have to dine on vomit and wallow in mud. Help me to keep my sincere mind stirred up and obey Your commandments. Amen.

DAY 46
TOWARDS GOD

"For my eyes are toward Thee, O God, the Lord; in Thee I take refuge; do not leave me defenseless."

(Psalm 141:8)

"Therefore, leaving the elementary teaching about the Christ, let us press on to maturity, not laying again a foundation of repentance from dead works and faith toward God..."

(Hebrews 6:1)

The lesson I have learned from these two passages, one from the Fat Part of the Book (The Old Testament) and one from the Skinny Part of the Book (The New Testament) is that my faith is directional and focused. My faith is not in—nor directed towards—my circumstances or situations. My faith is not in—nor directed towards—earthly solutions like politics, economics, world conditions (peace or unrest), nor in human beings (Christians or not Christians). Most definitely my faith is not in—nor directed inwardly toward—my own faith.

"Now faith is the assurance (the confirmation, the title-deed) of the things [we] hope for, being the proof of things [we] do not see and the conviction of their reality—faith perceiving as real fact what is not revealed to the senses."

(Hebrews 11:1/The Amplified Bible)

The psalmist once again cries out for protection against evil things, to those who practice deeds of wickedness along with iniquity doers. His eyes are not upon those things but toward the Lord. His eyes are toward the One in whom he will take refuge and his defense. As his eyes are toward the Lord, his voice is calling upon the Lord. For the believer who is going from a baby to a mature believer—who does not need milk but the meat of the Word—one of the basic, elementary principles of Christ is take that faith and direct it towards God.

> "Trust in the Lord (have your faith towards God) *with all your heart, and* do not lean on your own understanding."
> (Pro-Verbs 3:5, emphasis and addition mine)

There are times when you find yourself not trusting in the Lord and instead trusting in yourself or politics, economics, world conditions, other human beings, or even in your own faith. Whenever this happens in my life, soon as I begin to lean on my own understanding of these things, as soon as they shift or change, I fall over.

That is why you must direct your faith towards Him who will not shift or change as you have faith towards God. When your faith is toward God, it will change the way you approach life and deal with evil things, and wickedness, men of iniquity. The psalmist sings in Psalm 141:

- Calls upon the Lord for the Lord to hasten to him
- Asks the Lord to give ear to his voice
- Desires his prayer to be like incense before the Lord
- Lifts up his hands as an evening offering
- Wants his mouth guarded by the Lord
- Wants his lips to be watched over

PRAYER: Lord, I thank You that my faith is towards You and Your love is towards me. Amen.

DAY 47
WHO HAS?

"*Who has...?*"

(Pro-Verbs 23:29)

In this chapter, the pro-verbist continues with wisdom for the son that reaches into the future to give us some insights of positive actions for our life. There are six *"who has"* questions of cause-and-effect consequences in Pro-Verbs 23:31-35:

- Who has woe?
- Who has sorrow?
- Who has contentions?
- Who has complaining?
- Who has wounds without cause?
- Who has redness of eyes?

WOE: **'oy** (o'-ee)= Probably from H183 (in the sense of *crying* out after); *lamentation*; also interjectionally, *Oh*!: - alas, woe. **H183: 'avah** (aw-vaw')=A primitive root; to *wish* for: - covet, (greatly) desire, be desirous, long, lust (after). (*Strong's*)

NOTE: This word/phrase is associated with the Jewish people when they come up against something bad/negative as they cry out, "Oy Vay"!

SORROW: **'aboy** (ab-o'ee)=From H14 (in the sense of *desiring*); *want*:

- sorrow. **H14: 'abah** (aw-baw')=A primitive root; to *breathe* after, that is (figuratively) to *be acquiescent:* - consent, rest content, will, be willing. (*Strong's*)

CONTENTIONS: midyan (mid-yawn')=A variation for H4066: - brawling, contention (-ous). **H4066: mâdôn** (*maw-dohn'*)=; a *contest* or quarrel: - brawling, contention (-ous), discord, strife. (*Strong's*)

COMPLAINING/BABBLING: śıyach (see'-akh)=From H7878; a *contemplation*; by implication an *utterance:* - babbling, communication, complaint, meditation, prayer, talk. **H7878: śıyach** (see'-akh)=A primitive root; to *ponder*, that is, (by implication) *converse* (with oneself, and hence aloud) or (transitively) *utter:* - commune, complain, declare, meditate, muse, pray, speak, talk (with). (*Strong's*)

WOUNDS : petsaʻ (peh'-tsah)=From H6481; a *wound:* - wound (-ing). **H6481: patsaʻ** (paw-tsah')=A primitive root; to *split*, that is, *wound:* - wound. (*Strong's*)

WITHOUT CAUSE: chinnam (khin-nawm')=From H2580; *gratis*, that is, devoid of cost, reason or advantage: - without a cause (cost, wages), causeless, to cost nothing, free (-ly), innocent, for nothing (nought), in vain. **H2580: chen** (khane)= *graciousness*, that is, subjectively (*kindness, favor*) or objectively (*beauty*): - favour, grace (-ious), pleasant, precious, [well-] favoured. (*Strong's*)

REDNESS: chakliluth (khak-lee-looth')=From H2447; *flash* (of the eyes); in a bad sense, *blearedness:* - redness. **H2447: chaklıyl** (khak-leel')=By reduplication from an unused root apparently meaning to *be dark*; darkly *flashing* (only of the eyes); in a good sense, *brilliant* (as stimulated by wine): - red. (*Strong's*)

EYE: ʻayin (ah'-yin)=Probably a primitive word; an *eye* (literally or figuratively); by analogy a *fountain* (as the *eye* of the landscape): - affliction, outward appearance, + before, + think best, colour, conceit, + be content, countenance, + displease, eye ([-brow], [-d], -sight), face, + favour, fountain, furrow [from the margin], X him, + humble, knowledge, look, (+ well), X me, open (-ly), + (not) please, presence, + regard, resemblance, sight, X thee, X them, + think, X us, well, X you (-rselves). (*Strong's*)

That is a pretty long list of conditions and situations. The question is, *"Who has..."* these things. The pro-verbist reveals *"who has ..."* these things in Pro-Verbs 23:30-31:

- Those who linger long over wine.
- Those who go to taste (search out) mixed wine.
- Avoid wine when it is red, when it sparkles in the cup.
- The wine may go down smoothly.

WINE: Yayin (yah'-yin)=From an unused root meaning to effervesce; wine (as fermented); by implication intoxication: - banqueting, wine, wine [-bibber]. (*Strong's*)

MIXED WINE: mamsak (mam-sawk')=From H4537; *mixture*, that is, (specifically) wine *mixed* (with water or spices): - drink-offering, mixed wine. **H4537: masak (maw-sak')**=A primitive root; to mix, especially wine (with spices): - mingle. (*Strong's*)

I don't see a biblical prohibition in general for total abstinence, but I see over and over again that you should not get drunk. In our world, alcoholism is running rampant, with many claiming that they are not an alcoholic. There are a lot of people out there—Christians among them—who have woe, sorrow, contentions/babblings, wounds without cause, and redness of eyes. The current fad among believers is based on their freedom in Christ. They are free to drink, smoke, and even free to have sex outside of marriage. They say that are under grace and have the maturity to do certain things that the less mature Christians cannot do.

"All things are lawful for me, but not all things are profitable. All things are lawful for me, but I will not be mastered by anything."
(1 Corinthians 6:12)

"Therefore do not let/allow sin reign in your mortal body that you should obey its lusts, and do not go on presenting the members of your body to sin as instruments of unrighteousness; but present yourselves to God as those alive from the dead, and your members as instruments of righteousness to God."
(Romans 6:12-13)

Many times, people start out in freedom but end up in bondage. The cause-and-effect of the wine imbibing is:

- It goes down smoothly
- At the last it bites like a serpent
- It stings like a viper
- Your eyes will see strange things
- Your mind will utter perverse things
- You will be like one who lies down in the middle of the sea
- You will be like one who lies down on the top of a mast
- You will be struck but did not become ill
- You will be beaten but not know it
- When you will wonder when you wake up.
- You will seek yet again another drink.

"Who has...?"

PRAYER: Lord, thank You for my freedom, but thank You for the ability to resist, say no, and know when—or when not—to imbibe. Amen.

DAY 48
THE MOUNTAIN OF RETURN

"I will return to Zion, and dwell in the midst of Jerusalem. Jerusalem shall be called the City of Truth, The Mountain of the Lord of Hosts, the Holy Mountain."

(Zechariah 8:3)

The prophet Zechariah, in the book named after him, speaks forth words of encouragement and prophecy about rebuilding the Temple and of the coming Messiah. Theologians recognize that Zechariah ranks up there with the book of Isaiah in speaking of the coming Messiah.

There was the first coming of the Messiah when He entered the world in the form of a baby, in humble surroundings, in a small town, in a small country that was surrounded by bigger and more significant countries. This first coming of the Messiah included years of growth in wisdom, stature, and chronological progression to the ripe old age of thirty years.

Then, for three years, this Messiah/Christ demonstrated the kingdom and the will of God on earth as it was in Heaven. This Messiah came for the purpose of destroying the works of the d-evil and to atone for our sins as the propitiation, the satisfactory substitute for us on the cross. In this first coming, He is known as the "Suffering Messiah."

After He was crucified, buried, and rose again on the third day, He appeared to His followers for his final instructions before departure back to the Father. Some people call this the B.I.B.L.E.

B=BASIC
I=INSTRUCTION
B=BEFORE
L=LEAVING
E=EARTH

There is a Second Coming of the Messiah. It will be not in suffering but will be in power, greatness, and judgment and deliverance.

We need to be in preparation for this Second Coming as much as the people in Zechariah's time were in the rebuilding the Temple and in expectation for the coming Messiah. We need to be about the business of getting our lives in order, getting our lamps filled with fresh oil, and get those wicks trimmed and burning. In preparation for His leaving and instituting the B.I.B.L.E. Jesus left them.

When Jesus left in the clouds, His followers were encouraged that He would be back.

> *"And after He has said these things, He was lifted up while they were looking on, and a cloud received Him out of their sight. And as they were gazing intently into the sky while He was departing, behold, two men in white clothing stood beside them; and they also said, 'Men of Galilee, why do you stand looking into the sky? This Jesus, Who has been taken up from you into heaven, will come in just the same way as you have watched Him go into heaven.'"*
>
> (Acts 1:9-11)

> *"In that day His feet will stand on the Mount of Olives, which is in front of Jerusalem on the east; and the Mount of Olives will be split in its middle from east to west by a very large valley, so*

that half of the mountain will move toward the north and the other half toward the south."

(Zechariah 14:4)

"Behold, He is coming with the clouds, *and every eye will see Him, even those who pierced Him; and all the tribes of the earth will mourn over Him. So it is to be. Amen."*

(Revelation 1:7, emphasis mine)

Yes, Jesus is returning in the clouds just as He left. Yes, He will step onto the Mount of Olives as a conquering King. Yes, they will split into and become a source of exit for His people.

PRAYER: Lord, come quickly. Amen.

DAY 49
THE WRITTEN WRITING

> *"I am writing to you, little children...fathers...young men..."*
> (1 John 2:12-14)

John, the beloved disciple, wrote a Gospel and three epistles. The purpose of writing the Gospel was *so they could believe* (found 52 times) and the first Epistle of John (found 27 times in five chapters) was written *so they could know*.

> *"Jesus said to him, 'Because you have not seen Me, have you believed? Blessed are they who did not see, and yet believed.'" Many other signs therefore Jesus also performed in the presence of the disciples that are not written in this book; but these have been written, that you may believe that Jesus is the Christ, the Son of God; and that believing you may have life in His name."*
> (John 20:29-31)

BELIEVE: pisteuo (pist-yoo'-o)=From G4102; to *have faith* (in, upon, or with respect to, a person or thing), that is, *credit*; by implication to *entrust* (especially ones spiritual well-being to Christ): - believe (-r), commit (to trust), put in trust with. **G4102: pistis** (pis'-tis)=From G3982; *persuasion*, that is, *credence*; moral *conviction* (of *religious* truth, or the truthfulness of God or a religious teacher), especially *reliance* upon Christ for salvation; abstractly *constancy* in such profession; by extension the system of religious (Gospel) *truth* itself: - assurance, belief, believe, faith, fidelity. **G3982: peitho** (pi'-tho)=A primary verb; to *convince* (by argument, true or false); by analogy to *pacify* or *conciliate* (by other fair means); reflexively or passively to *assent* (to evidence or authority), to *rely* (by inward certainty): - agree, assure, believe, have confidence, be (wax) content, make friend, obey, persuade, trust, yield. (*Strong's*)

Again, in the first Epistle, the word *know* is found 27 times. You kind of get the idea that God wants you to *know* some things.

KNOW: eido (i'-d)=A primary verb; used only in certain past tenses, the others being borrowed from the equivalent properly to *see* (literally or figuratively); by implication (in the perfect only) to *know*: - be aware, behold, X can (+ not tell), consider, (have) known (-ledge), look (on), perceive, see, be sure, tell, understand, wist, wot. (*Strong's*)

The other phrases that jump out in 1 John is, *"I am writing…"* or *"I have written…"* These phrases occur 12 times within the five chapters. John has written things for specific purposes for the believing knowers. Today's devotional will be focusing on the reasons for the writing to the little children, fathers, and young men found in 1 John 2:12-14.

The three chronological categories include:

- Little children: Teknion (tek-nee'-on)=Diminutive of G5043; an *infant*, that is, (plural figurative) *darlings* (Christian *converts*): - little children. G5043: teknon (tek'-non)=; a *child* (as *produced*): - child, daughter, son. (*Strong's*)
- Fathers: patēr (pat-ayr')=Apparently a primary word; a father (literally or figuratively, near or more remote): - father, parent. (*Strong's*)
- Young men: neaniskos (neh-an-is'-kos)=From the same as G3494; a *youth* (under forty): - young man. G3494: neanias (*neh-an-ee'-as*)=From a derivative of G3501; a *youth* (up to about forty years): - young man. G3501: neos neōteros (*neh'-os, neh-*

o'-ter-os)=A primary word, including the comparative (second form); new, that is, (of persons) *youthful*, or (of things) *fresh*; figuratively *regenerate:* - new, young. (*Strong's*)

Now, here are the reasons why John is writing to the little children, fathers, and young men.

LITTLE CHILDREN: I am writing to you:

- That you may not sin
- If you do sin, realize you have an Advocate Who is the propitiation for our sins and the sins of the world
- Because your sins are forgiven for His name's sake
- Because you know the Father

FATHERS: I am writing to you:

- Because you know Him Who has been from the beginning
- Because you know Him Who has been from the beginning (this was written twice)

YOUNG MEN: I am writing to you:

- Because you have overcome the evil one
- Because you are strong
- Because the Word of God abides in you

All of these reasons for writing are hinged on the old commandment that is a new commandment.

> *"Beloved, I am not writing new commandment to you, but an old commandment which you have had from the beginning; the old commandment is the word which you have heard. On the other hand, I am writing a new commandment to you, which is true in*

Him and in you, because the darkness is passing away, and the true light is already shining."

(1 John 2:7-8)

That is love and not hate for your brothers/sisters in the Lord.

PRAYER: Lord, thank You for all the levels of growth in my life and how You have been there every step of the way. Amen.

DAY 50
THE CAVE OF DESPAIR

"When my spirit was overwhelmed within me, Thou didst know my path…"

(Psalm 142:3)

David was a man who was destined and anointed to be king, but was a man on the run from Saul. As his enemies pursued him, he took refuge in the caves of Adullam and Engedi. Both of those places turned into a place of prayer, a place of songs, a place of declaration, and a place fortified for temporary protection.

This was a place where David lamented, *"when my spirit was overwhelmed within me…"* (Psalm 142:3)

In this world, sometimes we have that sense of being overwhelmed and we need a place of release. Here is how David expressed his fears and frustration and the sense of trouble in his life.

- I cry aloud with my voice to the Lord.
- I make supplication with my voice to the Lord.
- I pour out my complaint before Him.
- I cried out to Thee, O Lord.
- I said, "Thou art my refuge.'
- Give heed to my cry.
- Deliver me from my persecutors.

- Bring my soul out of prison.

As he expressed himself, he stated:

> *"Look to the right and see; for there is no one who regards me; there is no escape for me; no one cares for my soul."*
>
> (Psalm 142:4)

Sometimes, we must get to the point where there is no natural help for us, and we must look up for some supernatural rescue and relief. When you are surrounded by hard rocks, dirt floor, and darkness, and the sound of the enemy echoes as they search for you, that is when the cave is turned into your prayer cathedral, sanctuary, and your refuge.

REFUGE: machaseh machseh (makh-as-eh', makh-seh')=From H2620; a *shelter* (literally or figuratively): - hope, (place of) refuge, shelter, trust. **H2620: chasah** (khaw-saw')=A primitive root; to *flee* for protection (compare H982); figuratively to *confide* in: - have hope, make refuge, (put) trust. (*Strong's*)

Not only did David cry out to the Lord and declare that the Lord is his shelter of hope, but also stated that the Lord was *"my portion."*

PORTION: cheleq (khay'-lek)=From H2505; properly *smoothness* (of the tongue); also an *allotment:* - flattery, inheritance, part, X partake, portion. **H2505: chalaq** (khaw-lak')=A primitive root; to *be smooth* (figuratively); by implication (as smooth stones were used for *lots*) to *apportion* or *separate:* - deal, distribute, divide, flatter, give, (have, im-) part (-ner), take away a portion, receive, separate self, (be) smooth (-er). (*Strong's*)

The Lord was David's refuge—not just in the sweet by-and-by—but in *"the land of the living."* This is where the bad stuff was happening. This is where the rough-and-tumble world was taking place. This was not the first time that David used this phrase.

> *"I would have despaired unless I had believed that I would see the goodness of the Lord in the land of the living."*
> (Psalm 27:13, emphasis mine)

This cave was like a soul prison that David needed to be released from so that he could fully give thanks to the Lord's name. In the place of lowness, the persecutors were too strong for him. Of course, this psalm of lament was for David at a specific time; but, as with many things in the Old Testament, they relate to us in our everyday walk.

PRAYER: Father, I come to You in the Name of Jesus in the land of the living. I need You and I will thank You for deliverance before I am released. Amen.

DAY 51
THE RISE AND FALL OF THE RIGHTEOUS MAN

> *"For a righteous man falls seven times, and rises again, but the wicked stumble in the time of calamity."*
>
> (Pro-Verbs 24:16)

Have you ever watched a baby learning to walk? How many babies have you seen who popped out of the womb, landed feet first on the floor, and immediately began to run marathons?

No, first they go from just laying around; to being able to turn over; to scooting around the floor; to getting up on hands and knees and crawling around; to pulling themselves up and wobbling and plopping down on their bottoms; to taking their first steps; and next thing you know, you are the one running the marathon around the house, trying to keep up with them. As that baby was in the process of learning to walk, he/she fell multiple times.

I experienced a fall recently at church. I was assisting a lady who was falling, and as I eased her down, my leg twisted and my knee popped. As the twist continued, my hamstrings hyper-extended and my left leg gave way. When that took place, my head/eyebrow slammed into a concrete floor covered with an indoor-outdoor kind of carpet with resultant carpet burn and black eye. The cause-and-effect was my glasses were wangled, my eyebrow was cut and bleeding and I was flat on my back in all kinds of pain.

As of this writing that was around two weeks ago and I am not still laying in the spot where I fell. I fell and rose up again. It may have been slowly, and I was still in pain, and it took a few days before I could begin to walk again, but I did "rise again."

The pro-verbist speaks of a "righteous man." I know that if I based my rising on my own righteousness, I would still be laying on that concrete church floor. According to Paul:

> *"there is none righteous, no not one."*
> (Romans 3:10, emphasis mine)

Paul also points out that:

> *"…we all have sinned and fallen short of the glory of God."*
> (Romans 3:23)

Based on these two verses, we are not righteous and we *do not have a leg to stand on*. What can get us to that status of a righteous man (or wo-man) where, when we fall, we can rise again? That is not based on anything we can do, but everything that He (Jesus) did.

Because Jesus died on the cross, was buried, and rose again from the dead, we are transitioned from unrighteousness to being a righteous man or wo-man *in Christ*.

> *"He made Him who knew no sin to be sin on our behalf that we might become the righteousness of God in Him."*
> (2 Corinthians 5:21)

Now when I fall, I don't have to just lay there. If I fall one time or seven times—or for that matter 490 times—I can rise again. Because He rose again one time on the third day, we can rise again no matter how many times we fall.

Once Peter was quizzing Jesus on how many times should we forgive someone. Then Peter threw out a number that he thought was rather liberal on the forgiveness scale of seven times.

PETER: *"...Lord, how often shall my brother sin against me and I forgive him up to seven times"?* (Matthew 18:22)

JESUS: *"...I do not say to you, up to seven times, but up to seventy times seven (490)."* (Matthew 18: 22, addition mine)

There is no need to hide the fact that we slipped, we stumbled, we fell, and we sinned because we are sinners.

> *"If we say that we have no sin, we are deceiving ourselves, and the truth is not in us. If we confess our sins, He is faithful and righteous and just to forgive us our sins and to cleanse us from all unrighteousness."*
>
> (1 John 1:8-9)

Are we sinners? Yes indeed. Are we righteous? In Christ, yes indeed! When (not if) we fall, should we just lay there forever? Indeed not! If He rose from the dead, surely in Him we rise again, and again, and again, and again.

PRAYER: Lord I have fallen down in the physical and I have fallen down in the spiritual. I thank You that each time, I rose again and continued on the path You have chosen for me to walk. Amen.

DAY 52
STICK 'EM UP GOD

"Will a man rob God? Yet you are robbing me! But you say, 'how have we robbed Thee...?'"
(Malachi 3:8)

I have a friend, brother in the Lord, co-laborer in the work of the Lord, who as Italian roots. Mario and I not only share a love of Italian Beef Sandwiches (wet), but we share our love for the Lord and His Word. My friend is astute in the ways of finance and teaches on the tithes, offerings, and giving in general. I love it when Mario teaches on the passage on tithing and in his best Italian voicing calls the book of Malachi the book of, "Muh la chee."

In the book of Malachi, the Temple had been rebuilt, the services within the Temple have been reestablished, but sin has raised its ugly head among the people once again. Now they were being accused of robbing God by God Himself. How were they robbing God?

"In tithes and contributions (heave offerings)*"*
(Malachi 3:8, emphasis mine)

The cause-and-effect of this robbery is a curse.

"You are cursed with a curse, for you are robbing Me, the whole nation of you!"
(Malachi 3:9)

In the Church, a big controversy has been raging for a long time.

- How much is a tithe?
- Are we required to tithe after the death, burial, and resurrection?
- Are we free not to tithe?
- Isn't tithing part of the Law?
- Did Jesus expect people to tithe?
- Where do I have to tithe?
- Just what and where is this thing called the storehouse?
- Is there a difference in tithing and giving a gift of money in an offering?
- Do I tithe on the gross or the net?
- Do I tithe on my income tax refund since I already tithed on the money I received in my paycheck?
- And the list goes on and on and on.

We are not going to answer or solve any of the questions or controversy in this book. After all, this is a devotional not a theological class on tithing.

Over the years, I have seen that a fool and his money may soon be parted; but a Christian and their money are not so easily pried loose. I have found that many have substituted the tithe with a tip like at tipping a waiter or waitress for good or bad service in our church service.

TITHE: ma'aśer ma'aśar ma'aśrah (mah-as-ayr', mah-as-ar', mah-as-raw')=From H6240; a *tenth*; especially a *tithe:* - tenth (part), tithe (-ing). **H6240: 'aśar** (w-sawr')= *ten* (only in combination), that is, the *"teens"*; also (ordinal) a *"teenth":* - [eigh-, fif-, four-, nine-, seven-, six-, thir-] teen (-th), + eleven (-th), + sixscore thousand, + twelve (-th) (*Strong's*)

The solution to the problem of Israel robbing God by robbing His tithes and contributions is found in the next verses, with not only the solution but the cause-and-effect of doing it.

- *Bring the whole tithe:* Not 1% or 5% or even 9% but 10%.
- *Into the storehouse:* A place to store whatever was brought in as a tithe. Some would say that the church is the storehouse but this is not reflected in the New Testament. However, I would say that if you are getting fed spiritually, then this could be the storehouse in your life. An example of giving your money elsewhere is like eating a certain eatery and then paying your bill at another eatery.
- *So that there may be food in My house:* God's house on the physical level was the Temple. God does not eat earthly food, but within His house He has staff/servants carrying on the business of the Temple.
- *Test Me now in this:* This is the only place where it is mentions to put God to a test (that I could find).
- *If I will not open for you the windows of Heaven:* This is the place where blessings flow. The old song says, "the windows of heaven are open, the blessings are falling tonight, there will be joy, joy, joy in my heart…"
- *And pour out for you a blessing until there is no more need:* The principle of seedtime/harvest, giving/ receiving, sowing/ reaping, cause-and-effect, reciprocity are implicated at this point.
- *Then I will rebuke the devourer for you:* The thing that would destroy what would be brought into the storehouse will be rebuked.
- *So that it may not destroy the fruits of the ground, nor will your vine in the field cast its grapes:* These represent the 10% that is being brought into the storehouse.
- *All the nations will call your blessed, for you shall be a delightful land:* People take notice when you are blessed.

I don't know about you, but I am feeling that I might need to let loose and let God do something in my life.

PRAYER: Lord, I don't know all the answers about money, but I do know that nothing I have is of my own making and it is Yours anyway.

Thank You for Your provision and thank You for letting me keep 90% of it. Amen.

DAY 53
WATCH WHAT YOU ARE DOING

"Watch yourselves that you might not lose what we have accomplished, but that you may receive a full reward."
(2 John 1:8)

In previous devotions gleaned from 2 John, we have looked at walking in love and the anti-Christ deceiver. To be honest with you, it is hard to continue to glean from an epistle that only has one chapter of only 13 verses. But we persevere, knowing that you could read one Word from God and see a multiplicity of truths.

Sometimes, as we are living our lives out by faith and not sight, we can relax our vigilance and things can sneak up on us. We might lose what we have accomplished and thus not receiving the full reward that God has for us. In the midst of deceivers gone out into the world, we need to keep up our guard and don't rely on others to watch out for us but to *"watch yourselves."*

WATCH: blepo (blep'-o)=A primary verb; to *look* at (literally or figuratively): - behold, beware, lie, look (on, to), perceive, regard, see, sight, take heed. (*Strong's*)

Larry Norman sang a song called *Watch What You're Doing*. The song states that if you are not careful and watch what you do, you can kill a chicken thinking it was a duck or even attempt to drown a cat that turned out to be a skunk. The bottom line of the song is that you really do have to watch what you're doing.

Believe it or not there are actually people out in the world who are out to get you and are trying to deceive you, just so they can deny you of what you have accomplished for the Lord. These people are described in 2 John 1:7.9:

- They do not acknowledge Jesus Christ as coming in the flesh (came from heaven and physically took the form of a human).
- They are deceivers and the antichrist,
- They do not abide in the teaching of Christ.
- They do not have God.

In another verse of the same song by Larry Norman, he warns us about people who smile but turn out to be angels of light and tells us to love everybody with our eyes wide open, because they will try to mess with your mind. Not only do you have to watch what you're doing but you must watch who you know.

You have to be careful, watchful, and on guard. How should you respond to these people? It is recommended in 2 John 1:8, 10-11:

- Watch yourselves
- If they come to you do not receive him into your house
- Do not give him a greeting unless you want to participate in his evil deeds.

At Bill Taylor's Bushido School of Karate, where I take and teach karate, Mr. Taylor has some good insights on how to keep your awareness up in these dangerous times. He uses The Color Code of Awareness. There is a Japanese word called *Zanshin* that means *the awareness of your surroundings*. Here is the color code Mr. Taylor uses, which can be valuable for our spiritual watching of ourselves.

THE COLOR CODE OF AWARENESS

- WHITE: This is what most people walk in their everyday life. It is like they have tunnel vision focused on what they need to accomplish and not looking around them. They are not "watching themselves."
- YELLOW: This is someone who is more aware and they are using more caution. This is known as a pre-emptive mode as they scan their surroundings and notice anybody that may be out of the ordinary.
- RED: This is someone with even more awareness and they are sensing a problem and are alerting themselves of how they might need to adjust what they are doing or where they are going in case of an attack.
- BLACK: This is where you are actually under attack. If you had yellow and red in operation, you may not have to be in the black mode. In this mode, you will have to make adjustments in fighting and/or trying to get help.

THE COLOR CODE OF SPIRITUAL AWARENESS

- WHITE: This is when you go through the world blindly trusting anyone who comes along, and do not think that there are people who are antichrist and deceivers, or that there is a d-evil—or if there is--he does not have schemes against them and will be leaving them alone. These people are susceptible to deceivers.
- YELLOW: These people are more spiritually aware and use caution when people come to them quoting scriptures or giving them prophecy to guide their lives. They realize that like Jesus realized that everyone who says "Lord, Lord" is not necessarily a follower of Christ, and Jesus would tell them, "I never knew you."
- RED: This is someone even more spiritually aware, with their

spiritual radar set on high alert. They might have what the world would call gut feeling, but what we know is the Holy Spirit guarding and warning us. For both yellow and red, you must have a renewed mind, so that when the attacks of falsehoods come, you will know the Truth. As Jesus defined truth, *"...Thy Word is truth."* (John 17:17)

- BLACK: It is not *"if"* you come under attack, but it is a matter of *"when"* you will come under demonic attack by the d-evil. He has well-orchestrated schemes of attacks against you. (Ephesians 6:11-13) Jesus was tempted in the wilderness but utilize the Holy Spirit, the Word of God, and the authority of the Father to win the battle. Once the d-evil eases up, you have to keep guard and stand after you have done everything. (Ephesians 6:10-11, 13) When the d-evil had finished every temptation against Jesus, he departed from Him *until an opportune time.* (Luke 4:13) This means that once you win a battle, keep your guard up, watch yourselves, and stand. Keep the color code of awareness activated. It is like your virus protection on your computer; don't shut of the virus protection after it catches a virus stay on guard.
- Wow, for such a small chapter and verse. we covered a lot of territory.

PRAYER: Lord, thank You for the ability to be aware and realize when it is the enemy is on the move in my life. Amen.

DAY 54

THE SCHOOL OF THY WILL

"Teach me to do Thy will, for Thou art my God; let Thy good Spirit lead me on level ground."

(Psalm 143:10)

TEACH: lamad (law-mad')=A primitive root; properly to *goad*, that is, (by implication) to *teach* (the rod being an Oriental *incentive*): - [un-] accustomed, X diligently, expert, instruct, learn, skilful, teach (-er, -ing). (*Strong's*)

I find it interesting that the concept of the Lord teaching the psalmist is to be *goaded on with a rod* as incentive to do the will of God. Then again, I find myself needing some extra encouragement when I am trying to follow His will on earth as it is in Heaven. God is the Headmaster; the Holy Spirit is the one who teaches and leads us; and Jesus is the Word and example of how to be obedient to the Father as a servant. The psalmist is not saying to teach him God's will, but to teach him *"to do Thy will."*

WILL: ratson ratson (raw-tsone', raw-tsone')=From H7521; *delight*: - (be) acceptable (-ance, -ed), delight, desire, favour, (good) pleasure, (own, self, voluntary) will, as . . . (what) would. **H7521: ratsah** (raw-tsaw')=A primitive root; to *be pleased with*; specifically to *satisfy* a debt: - (be) accept (-able), accomplish, set affection, approve, consent with, delight (self), enjoy, (be, have a) favour (-able), like, observe, pardon, (be, have, take) please (-ure), reconcile self. (*Strong's*)

When Jesus' disciples asked Him to teach them how to pray like John the Baptist taught his disciple. Jesus taught them what is known as "The Lord's Prayer," which was really not *His* prayer but the prayer for them to pray. The true "Lord's prayer" is found in John, Chapter 17. Jesus taught them, certain things to pray and one of them was to pray that:

> *"Thy will be done on earth as it is in Heaven."*
> (Matthew 6:10)

This correlates with the psalmist's desire to be taught to *"do Thy will."* (Psalm 143:10) Who will be doing this teaching? The psalmist asks that God's good Spirit (aka The Holy Spirit) to lead him on a level ground as He teaches him to *"do Thy will."* (Psalm 143:10)

LEAD: nachah (naw-khaw')=A primitive root; to *guide*; by implication to *transport* (into exile, or as colonists): - bestow, bring, govern, guide, lead (forth), put, straiten. (*Strong's*)

> *"But the Helper, the Holy Spirit, Whom the Father will send in My name, He will teach you all things, and bring to your remembrance all that I said to you."*
> (John 14:26)

TEACH: didasko (did-as'-ko)=A prolonged (causative) form of a primary verb δάω daō (to *learn*); to *teach* (in the same broad application): - teach. (*Strong's*)

BRING: hupomimnesko (hoop-om-im-nace'-ko)=; to *remind quietly*, that is, *suggest* to the (middle voice, ones own) memory: - put in mind, remember, bring to (put in) remembrance. (*Strong's*)

The psalmist requested the Holy Spirit to lead him on level ground. As believers, we also have the Holy Spirit teacher *dwelling inside of us with the anointing to teach us.*

"As for you, the anointing which you received from Him abides in you, and you have no need for anyone to teach you; but as His anointing teaches you about all things, and is true and is not a lie, and just as it has taught you, you abide in Him."

(1 John 2:27)

ANOINTING: Chrisma (khris'-mah**)**=From G5548; an *unguent* or *smearing*, that is, (figuratively) the special *endowment* ("chrism") of the Holy Spirit: - anointing, unction. **G5548: chrio (**khree'-o**)**= the idea of *contact*; to *smear* or *rub* with oil, that is, (by implication) to *consecrate* to an office or religious service: - anoint. (*Strong's*)

PRAYER: Lord, thank You for the indwelling Holy Teacher. Thank You that Your Holy Spirit teaches me all things, including not only Your will, but actually how to do Your will on earth as it is in Heaven. Amen.

DAY 55
A CHUNKA CHUNKA OF BURNING COALS

"For you will heap burning coals on his head, and the Lord will reward you."

(Pro-Verbs 25:22)

Back in the 50's Elvis Presley had a hit song called, *A Big Hunka Love*. Fast forward to 1972, where Elvis released a song called Burning Love. It was rocketing to # 1 on the Billboard charts and was on the road to becoming his biggest hit since *Suspicious Minds* in 1969.

The problem was that it stalled at #2 because a novelty song by Chuck Berry called *My Ding-a-Ling*. Elvis sang the phrase that was a tip of the hat to *A Big Hunka Love* with the phrase, ""A hunk-a-hunk-a of burning love"

Speaking of burning love, the psalmist speaks of burning coals that are heaped on top of an enemies' head and the cause-and-effect of acts of kindness.

"If your enemy is hungry, give him food to eat; and if he is thirsty, give him water to drink..."

(Pro-Verbs 25:21)

These acts of kindness are what your enemy is not expecting. Talk about taking them by surprise. The expected response to an enemies' needs would be to allow them to go hungry and thirsty to the point of death. You have the upper hand on your enemy and vengeance will be yours. Of course, God has a better way and is voiced in Paul's letter to the Romans.

> *"Never pay back evil for evil to anyone. Respect what is right in the sight of all men. If possible, so far as it depends on you, be at peace with all men. Never take your own revenge, beloved, but leave room for the wrath of God for it is written, 'Vengeance is Mine, I will repay,' says the Lord. But if your enemy is hungry, feed him, and if he is thirsty, give him a drink; for in doing so you will heap burning coals upon his head.' Do not be overcome by evil, but overcome evil with good."*
>
> (Romans 12:17-21)

In the Pro-Verb passage, the cause-and-effect is a reward from the Lord; in the Romans passage, there is repayment from the Lord. Showing kindness by not paying back what is deserved; showing respect in the sight of all men; and not taking your own revenge has the cause-and-effect of leaving room for the wrath of God.

I have found that when I do not leave room for the wrath of God, I cut God out of helping me with my problems. I may get temporary satisfaction with the wrath of Rod, but the same problems will continue to plague me over and over again. When I leave room for the wrath of God, however, it opens the doors for coals of fire on the enemies' head, or as the title of this devotion states, "a chunka chunk of burning coals." The Romans passage lays it out this way:

- Never pay back evil for evil to anyone
- Respect what is right in the sight of all men
- Be at peace with all men as far as it depends on you, if possible (it may not be)
- Never take your own revenge

- Leave room for the wrath of God
- Don't be overcome by evil
- Overcome evil with good

I read this, and I agree that this is how I should act, but I also have to be honest and say that I fall short of this standard. I know in my own flesh I can't do it, but in the Spirit, I can do all things, because with man it is impossible but with God it is possible.

PRAYER: Lord, help me. Amen.

DAY 56
400 SILENT AND DARK YEARS

"There is an appointed time for everything and there is a time for every event under heaven...a time to be silent, and a time to speak."

(Ecclesiastes 3:1; 7)

SILENT/SILENCE: chashah (khaw-shaw')=A primitive root; to *hush* or keep quiet: - hold peace, keep silence, be silent, (be) still. (*Strong's*)

As the book of Malachi closes out with the prophet giving a word of repentance for the people and the promise of a Messiah with covenant promises fulfilled, the times became dark and silent for 400 years. I don't know why there was 400 years of silence concerning God moving and speaking. Although I have no evidence, I believe that God was still moving.

During this silent period, the world was changing, sinners were still sinning, the political and economic climate was shifting until there was a breakthrough in the silence with another prophet who was proclaiming the coming Messiah. A man from the Qumran community of a sect of people called the Essenes appeared in the wilderness crying out:

"Repent, for the kingdom of heaven is at hand."

(Matthew 3:2)

This was proclamation and declaration of a Light that would shine in the darkness. It would mark the entrance of Jesus the Christ, God in the flesh, the Light of the World manifesting the will of God on Earth as it was in Heaven.

> *"In the beginning was the Word (Jesus) and the Word (Jesus) was with God, and the Word (Jesus) was God. He was in the beginning with God. All things came into being through Him (Jesus); and apart from Him (Jesus) nothing came into being that has come into being. In Him (Jesus) was the life; and the life was the light of men. And the light shines in the darkness; and the darkness did not comprehend it."*
>
> (John 1:1-5, addition mine)

Out of the silent darkness came the light.

> *"There was the true light which, coming into the world enlightens every man."*
>
> (John 1:9)

> *"The land of Zebulun and the land of Naphtali, by the way of the sea, beyond the Jordan, Galilee of the Gentiles---the people who were sitting in darkness saw a great light, and those who were sitting in the land and shadow of death upon them a light dawned."*
>
> (Matthew 4:15-17, Isaiah 9:1-2)

Yes, in those dark and silent days there would be an incubation of noise and light that would put to silence the ignorant and arrogant. Messiah would be revealed with His first coming as a baby and suffering Messiah and then—the second time—as the resurrected and victorious King of Kings and Lord of Lords.

Even today, men and women claim that God is dead or that He is still silent and does not—or will not, or cannot—speak to His creation any longer. The philosopher Francis Schaffer wrote a book *He is Not Silent*, and the Christian music duo Out of the Grey sang based on the Schaffer book. In both book and song, it was stated that, while it may appear that God is silent, He is not. The problem is our selective hearing; we don't listen to Him. Even if He does sent help, we tend to resist that help.

There may have been 400 dark and silent years, but now for 2000 years the light is on and the volume is turned up.

PRAYER: Lord, I hear You loud and clear. Amen.

DAY 57
THE SINCEREST FORM OF FLATTERY

"Beloved, do not imitate what is evil, but what is good. The one who does good is of God, the one who does evil has not seen God."

(3 John 1:11)

IMITATE: Mimeomai (mim-eh'-om-ahee)=Middle voice from μιμος mimos (a mimic); to *imitate:* - follow. (*Strong's*)

I love to listen and watch people who are impersonators. They have honed their skills where they can mimic the vocal quality and mannerisms of some well-known people. Back in my day, there were people like Rich Little and Frank Gorshin, Sammy Davis Jr., and in this day and age people like Frank Caleindo, Steve Bridges, and many more on late night comedy shows. Every once in a while, I will attempt an impersonation or two. Who has not said, "Thank ya', thank ya' very much," and think they sound just like Elvis?

As the title of today's devotion states, people do believe that imitation is the sincerest form of flattery. That is, unless they are mocking you.

John is writing a letter, encouraging believers to continue in hospitality and sharing with those who are traveling as fellow-workers for the Gospel. In the letter, John commends Gaius and Demetrius and he rebukes Diotrephes.

In respect to the way they treat people, Gaius and Demetrius are the good ones and are of God, while Diotrephes is the evil one and has not seen God. Two are to be imitated and the other is not to be imitated. Diotrephes:

EVIL (3 John 1:8-10)

- Loves to be first among them
- Does not accept what John has to say
- Unjustly accuses John
- Speaks wicked words concerning John
- He does not receive the brethren (no hospitality)
- Forbids those who desire to receive the brethren (show hospitality) to do so
- Puts those needing hospitality out of the church

Diotrephes is who and what you are not to imitate. Why? He is evil.

What about Gaius and Demetrius who are not evil but do the good that John encouraged the church to imitate?

GOOD (3 John 1:3-8, 12)

- Walking in the truth
- Acting faithfully in whatever is accomplished for the brethren and strangers
- Their love is observable
- Acts in a manner worthy of God
- Supports fellow-workers of the truth
- Received a good testimony from everyone
- Received a good testimony from the truth itself

Imitating human beings could be good or it could be bad, depending on whether what they are doing at the moment is good or bad. Paul encourages them—and us—to imitate someone who will never fall short of the mark.

> *"Therefore be imitators of God, as beloved children; and walk in love, just as Christ also loved you and gave Himself up for us, an offering and a sacrifice to God as a fragrant aroma."*
>
> (Ephesians 5:1)

In various places in the New Testament, Paul encourages people to be imitators (followers) of him. I wonder if I want people to imitate/follow me? Here are a few more verses to underscore imitation.

- 1 Corinthians 4:16: Imitate/follow me (Paul)
- 1 Corinthians 11:1: Imitate/follow me (Paul) as I am of Christ
- Ephesians 5:1: Imitate/follow God
- Philippians 3:17: Imitate/follow us as examples (a die, struck/cast in shape and form)
- 1 Thessalonians 1:6: Imitate/follow us and The Lord
- 1 Thessalonians 2:14: Imitate/follow the churches of God in Christ Jesus
- Hebrews 6:12: Imitate/follow those who through faith and patience inherit the promise
- 1 Peter 3:13: Imitate/follow/be zealous: for what is good
- 3 John 1:11: Imitate/follow that which is good

When Paul was imprisoned in Rome, he told the church in Philippi to let/allow you minds to dwell on whatever is:

- true
- honorable
- right
- pure
- lovely
- of good report

- has any excellence
- has anything worthy of praise

Paul then told them about the things that they had:

- learned
- received
- heard
- seen in him
- practiced (being imitators of Paul)

The cause-and-effect is that:

> *"...the God of peace shall be with you."*
> (Philippians 4:9)

PRAYER: Lord, I thank You that we have examples to follow and imitate, all based on Your nature and character. Amen.

DAY 58
THE BLESSED SITUATION

"How blessed are the people who are so situated; how blessed are the people whose God is the Lord!"

(Psalm 144:15)

When I hear the word *situation*, I generally think of a condition—or state of affairs and circumstances—that is in a negative light. When someone is in trouble with their backs against the wall we might say, "They are in a bad situation."

This use to confuse me back in the 70's, when we would sing a song based on Psalm 48, *Great is the Lord* and the phrase came up, "beautiful for situation."

I would think, *How can having your back against the wall in conditions, state of affairs, and circumstances be beautiful?* That was until I realized that Psalm 48 was singing about the greatness of the Lord, the fact that He is worthy to be praised. The city of God was high on a mountain and, as we come to the mountain, we are situated in a high place to be able to see from a God's eye view.

The phrase "beautiful for situation" means a position of elevation. This situation or elevation is a place where you can have a God's-eye view of all below and a view of enemies who may try to surround the city or ascend up to take captive the city.

Another thing I noticed is that the word *situation* was singular and not plural with situation(s). Psalm 144 starts with the declaration:

> *"Blessed be the Lord, my rock, Who trains my hands for war, and my fingers for battle..."*
>
> (Psalm 144:1)

Then the psalmist declares that His Lord is His:

- lovingkindness
- fortress
- stronghold
- deliverer
- shield
- refuge

When the enemy surrounds the psalmist, he has a God's-eye view because of the blessing of being situated and elevated.

We, as believers in the Death, Burial and Resurrection (D.B.R.) of Jesus the Christ, the Anointed One, have a new perspective on life. While we still live here on planet Earth, as we have been raised up (elevated) with Christ.

> *"If then you have been raised up with Christ, keep seeking the things above where Christ is seated at the right hand of God. Set your mind on the things above, not on the things that are on the earth. For you have died and your life is hidden with Christ in God."*
>
> (Colossians 3:1-3)

In a lost and dying and dangerous world we have to have "situated eyes." We have to have a "God's-eyed view." While the world falls apart, we are able to declare that *"great is the Lord."* Why can we declare that? We can declare that because we are blessed people who are *"so situated"* and it is *"beautiful for situation."*

PRAYER: Lord, thank You for being positioned and situated in Christ where I can see things through eyes of faith and not fear. Amen.

DAY 59
DID YOU HEAR THE ONE ABOUT FIREBRANDS AND DEATH?

"Like a madman who throws firebrands, arrows, and death, so is the man who deceives his neighbor, and says, 'Was I not joking?'"
(Pro-Verbs 26:18-19)

Have you ever heard—or have you ever said—something that was hurtful to someone but added, "I'm only kidding?"

Sometimes the most hurtful things can be said under the guise of humor. People may say that they did not mean what they said, but the hurt is done and the weapon is hidden under a joke.

My friend Bill Combs is the one who pointed this out to me because I was famous for my quick wit (in my own mind), funny puns (again in my own mind), my sharp sarcasm (really dull), and my ability to make people laugh while I insulted them and then pull the, "Just kidding" line. Whether I was kidding or not, the damage was already done. Once you shoot a gun, you can't bring back the bullet by being sorry. So it is when you shoot off your mouth; "Just kidding" does not ease the hurt, accidental or intentional.

MAD: lahahh (law-hah')=A primitive root meaning properly to *burn*, that is, (by implication) to *be rabid* (figuratively *insane*); also (from the *exhaustion* of frenzy) to *languish:* - faint, mad. (*Strong's*)

When we say *madman*, we are not necessarily referencing someone of the male species who is angry and upset as much as a crazy man. This madman is armed with something more than deadly firebrands and arrows of the biblical days, or in this day and age, bullets.

FIREBRANDS: zıyqah ziq zeq (zee-kaw', zeek, zake)=From H2187; properly what *leaps* forth, that is, *flash* of fire, or a burning *arrow*; also (from the original sense of the root) a *bond:* - chain, fetter, firebrand, spark. **H2187: zanaq (**zaw-nak')=A primitive root; properly to *draw together* the feet (as an animal about to dart upon its prey), that is, to *spring* forward: - leap. (*Strong's*)

ARROWS: chets (khayts)=From H2686; properly a *piercer*, that is, an *arrow*; by implication a *wound*; figuratively (of God) thunder *bolt*; the *shaft* of a spear: - + archer, arrow, dart, shaft, staff, wound. **H2686: chatsats (**khaw-tsats')=A primitive root (compare H2673); properly to *chop* into, pierce or sever; hence to *curtail*, to *distribute* (into ranks); to *shoot* an arrow: - archer, X bands, cut off in the midst. (*Strong's*)

DEATH: chatsats (khaw-tsats')= properly to *chop* into, pierce or sever; hence to *curtail*, to *distribute* (into ranks);; to *shoot* an arrow: - archer, X bands, cut off in the midst. (*Strong's*)

It is interesting that the word *man* in *madman* is rooted in the word *to burn*, which refers to the nature of his weapons as burning, piercing instruments of death. The weapons are of a stealth nature, hidden so as not to be immediately detected, just as the deception of death is hidden in a joke.

JOKING: śachaq (saw-khak')=A primitive root; to *laugh* (in pleasure or detraction); by implication to *play:* - deride, have in derision, laugh, make merry, mock (-er), play, rejoice, (laugh to) scorn, be in (make) sport. (*Strong's*)

It is also interesting that a part of the d-evil's arsenal towards us is a *"flaming missile of the evil one."* (Ephesians 6:16)

The launching mechanisms for the firebrands/arrows/death are found in the mouth, which is a reflection of the mind.

> *"Death and life are in the power of the tongue, and those who love it will eat its fruit."*
> (Pro-Verbs 18:21)

As the context flows in Pro-Verbs 26:20-21, we see:

- For lack of wood, the fire goes out.
- Where there is no whisperer, contention quiets down.
- Like charcoal to hot embers and wood to fire, so is a contentious man to kindle strife.

It may be time to remove the fire from the firebrands, arrows, and death, and let the fire die down on those flaming jokes.

PRAYER: Father, help me to guard my tongue, my lips, my mouth, my words. Amen.

DAY 60
THE LAUGH OF LOVE

"And Sarah laughed to herself (within) saying, 'After I have become old, shall I have pleasure, my lord (Abraham) being old also?'"

(Genesis 18:12, addition mine)

LAUGHED: tsachaq (tsaw-khak)=A primitive root; to *laugh* outright (in merriment or scorn); by implication to *sport:* - laugh, mock, play, make sport. (*Strong's*)

This word can be used with merriment, where you laugh when something tickles the "funny bone." Or it can be used with scorn where something tickles the "I cannot believe it bone." In Sarah's case, it is it is the "scorn bone."

Abraham had a promise from God that was for him in his lifetime and would extend to the world. He was promised a child and, in addition, that the stars/sand could not be numbered with his children of promise. This is predicting the appearance of Jesus, Who would be the Savior of the world. The problem is that, if there is no child born to Abraham and Sarah, then there would be no Jesus and thus no blessing to the world.

We will always have an opportunity to either laugh in scorn or laugh in joy when God is about to do the impossible in our lives. The angel came to Mary and gave her the news of the impossibility that God was about to do in her life. She responded by questioning how it can happen since she was a virgin and never had sexual relations with a man.

> *"And Mary said to the angel, 'How can this be since I am a virgin.'"*
> (Luke 1:34)

Mary was at a crossroad, where she could either laugh in scorn or laugh in joy. First, however, first she had to yield her will and logic to faith.

The angel spoke about the impossibility.

> *"For nothing will be impossible with God."*
> (Luke 1:37)

> *"And Mary said, 'Behold, the bond-slave of the Lord; be it done to me according to your word.' And the angel departed from her."*
> (Luke 1:38)

This acceptance of the Word of the Lord, delivered by the messenger of the Lord, leads her to exalting and rejoicing. I imagine—and this is my own thought—that within that exalting and rejoicing, there was joy springing up with the laugh of love on her lips.

> *"And blessed is she who believed that there would be a fulfillment of what had been spoken to her by the Lord. And Mary said: 'My soul exalts the Lord, and my spirit has rejoiced in God my Savior.'"*
> (Luke 1:45-46)

In the promise given to Abraham and Sarah, she was at the door of the tent, listening to the word that the strangers prophetically spoke to Abraham.

> *"And he said, 'I will surely return to you at this time next year; and behold, Sarah your wife shall have a son'. And Sarah was listening at the tent door, which was behind him. Now Abraham and Sarah were old, advanced in age; Sarah was past childbearing."*
>
> (Genesis 18:10-11)

Just like Mary, Sarah had a chance to doubt or believe. She chose to laugh in scorn.

> *"And Sarah laughed to herself, saying, 'After I have become old, shall I have pleasure, my lord being old also?'"*
>
> (Genesis 18:12)

The facts were real. These facts are reflected by Paul in Romans.

> *"And without becoming weak in faith he (Abraham) contemplated his own body (took stock of his physical being), now as good as dead since he was about a hundred years old, and the deadness of Sarah's womb."*
>
> (Romans 4:19, addition mine)

As Sarah was laughing away about the impossibility of her bearing a child, the Lord—Was the angel—questioned Abraham about Sarah.

> *"And the Lord said to Abraham, 'Why did Sarah laugh, saying shall I indeed bear a child when I am so old.'"*
>
> (Genesis 18:13)

As the angel did with Mary in Luke 1, the stranger/angel/Lord then underscored with Sarah about impossibilities.

> *"'Is anything too difficult for the Lord? At the appointed time I will return to you, at this time next year, and Sarah shall have a son.'"*
>
> (Genesis 18:14)

The answer was—and is—*No, nothing is too difficult for the Lord.* Sarah was still in the denial mode, but He called her on it and said that she did laugh.

I like the fact that, even in unbelief, God was gracious to Abraham and Sarah, even in the face of her laughing scorn. He laughed back with the laughter of love.

PRAYER: Lord, I believe; help Thou my unbelief and my laughter of unbelief. Thank You for mercy. Amen.

DAY 61
JUST A REMINDER

> *"Now I desire to remind you, though you know all things once for all that the Lord, after saving a people out of the land of Egypt, subsequently destroyed those who did not believe."*
>
> (Jude 1:5)

This is a small book of one chapter of 25 verses. I must admit that it is hard to glean something from Jude, as this is my third visit to the well. The bulk of the book is warning about people and angels who would attempt to pull believers away from the truth. Isn't that how our God is? While we are in sin and rebellion, He would send prophets with warnings and encouragement.

As I study the Bible, I find various verses, chapters, or books that complement each other. For this verse, I see a correlation in 1 Corinthians 10, as Paul speaks twice of what happened to these people who were saved out of the land of Egypt but were, "laid low in the wilderness."

> *"Nevertheless, with most of them, God was not well pleased; for they were laid low in the wilderness."*
>
> (1 Corinthians 10:5)

> *"Now these things happened as examples for us, that we should not crave evil things as they also craved."*
>
> (1 Corinthians 10:6)

"Now these things happened to them as an example, and they were written for our instruction, upon whom the ends of the ages have come."
(1 Corinthians 10:11)

What laid these people low in the wilderness that subsequently destroyed them? What brought them to such a low estate? In 1 Corinthians 10:7-10 we see:

- They craved evil things (lusts)
- They were idolaters (worshipped someone other than God)
- The sat down to eat and drink, and stood up to play (partiers)
- They acted immorally (going against God's principles)
- They tried the Lord (selfishly tested God and pushed Him to the limit)
- They grumbled (griped, complained, moaned and groaned, kvetched)

They were warned and—as in Jude—reminded. Arrogant minded men and women think that they can get away with things. They try to see how close to the edge of the river of sin can they get and not slip in. Paul gives the warning:

"Therefore, let him who thinks he stands take heed lest he fall."
(1 Corinthians 10:12)

PRAYER: Lord, thanks for the reminder and warnings. I hear You loud and clear Lord. Amen.

DAY 62
THE LORD IS:

"Great is the Lord, and highly to be praised; and His greatness is unsearchable."

(Psalm 145:3)

In my Bible, under Psalm 145, the phrase, *The Lord Extoled for His Goodness* is listed as *A Psalm of Praise of David*. What jumps out at me is the phrase, "the Lord is." The psalmist declares in the first verse that:

"I will extol Thee, my God, O King; and I will bless Thy name forever and ever."

(Psalm 145:1)

That has been accomplished, as the Psalms were considered to be written 1410-450 B.C., and here we are, some two thousand years later, joining in the extolling the Lord and His marvelous attributes.

For today's reading, we will look at why the Lord is so great and why the Lord is highly to be praised because of His unsearchable greatness.

EXTOL: rum (room)= A primitive root; to *be high* actively to *rise* or *raise* (in various applications, literally or figuratively): - bring up, exalt (self), extol, give, go up, haughty, heave (up), (be, lift up on, make on, set up on, too) high (-er, one), hold up, levy, lift (-er) up, (be) lofty, (X a-) loud, mount up, offer (up), + presumptuously, (be) promote (-ion), proud, set up, tall (-er), take (away, off, up), breed worms. (*Strong's*)

BLESS: barak (baw-rak')=A primitive root; to *kneel*; by implication to *bless* God (as an act of adoration), and (vice-versa) man (as a benefit); also (by euphemism) to *curse* (God or the king, as treason): - X abundantly, X altogether, X at all, blaspheme, bless, congratulate, curse, X greatly, X indeed, kneel (down), praise, salute, X still, thank. (*Strong's*)

The psalmist states in Psalm 145:1-7, and we do also:

- I will extol Thee.
- I will bless Thy name forever and ever.
- Every day I will bless Thee.
- I will praise Thy name forever and ever.
- Great is the Lord and highly to be praised.
- On Thy wonderful works, I will meditate.
- I will speak along with other men of the power/strength of Thy awesome acts.
- I will tell of Thy greatness.
- They shall eagerly utter the memory of Thine abundant goodness.
- They shall shout joyfully of Thy righteousness.

The psalmist now shifts and begins to do what he said that he would do concerning the Lord. He sings in Psalm 145:8-20

The Lord is:

- Gracious
- Merciful
- Slow to anger
- Great in lovingkindness
- Good to all
- His mercies are over all His works

- Sustains all who fall
- Raises up all who are bowed down
- Give them their food in due time
- Opens Thy hand
- Satisfies the desire of every living thing.
- Righteous in all His ways
- Kind in all His deeds
- Near to all who call upon Him in truth
- Fulfills the desire of those who fear Him
- Hears the cry and will save them
- Keeps all who love Him

The psalmist ends by say what will take place because of all the wonderful attributes that we have listed.

> *"My mouth will speak the praise of the Lord; and all flesh will bless His holy name forever and ever."*
> (Psalm 145: 21)

We might as well get started on speaking praise and blessing His name, because forever and ever is a long time.

PRAYER: Lord I join in on extolling You and blessing Your name forever and ever. Amen.

DAY 63
HUSBANDRY AND AGRICULTURE 101

"Know well the condition of your flocks and pay attention to your herds."

(Pro-Verbs 27:23)

Flocks and herds and fields represent the livelihood and sustenance for the farmers of the day. Even Adam and Eve were called to tend the Garden which they were given. (Genesis 2:15) They were to cultivate and keep it.

CULTIVATE/DRESS: 'abad (aw-bad') = A primitive root; to *work* (in any sense); by implication to *serve, till,* (causatively) *enslave,* etc.: - X be, keep in bondage, be bondmen, bond-service, compel, do, dress, ear, execute, + husbandman, keep, labour (-ing man), bring to pass, (cause to, make to) serve (-ing, self), (be, become) servant (-s), do (use) service, till (-er), transgress [from margin], (set a) work, be wrought, worshipper. (*Strong's*)

KEEP: shamar (shaw-mar') = A primitive root; properly to *hedge* about (as with thorns), that is, *guard*; generally to *protect, attend to,* etc.: - beware, be circumspect, take heed (to self), keep (-er, self), mark, look narrowly, observe, preserve, regard, reserve, save (self), sure, (that lay) wait (for), watch (-man). (*Strong's*)

The verse for today speaks of knowing the condition of your flocks and herds. In the Genesis passage Adam was commissioned to cultivate and keep the Garden, but I believe this goes deeper than just animals and vegetables. I believe it speaks to our own human and spiritual condition. We need to know the condition of our spirit, soul, and body and we are to cultivate and keep the garden of our being as humans. Psalm 37:3 speaks of this.

> *"Trust in the Lord and do good; dwell in the land and cultivate faithfulness."*
>
> (Psalm 37:3)

In the margin of my Bible that word *cultivate* means to: (1) feed securely (2) feed on His faithfulness. This is the only way that you can do this: (1) know (2) pay attention to your spiritual condition.

There will be reward and provision if you do these things in the natural and in your supernatural/spiritual. In this Pro-verb (Positive Action), we see some insights into the cause-and-effect of knowing the condition and paying attention to things. Pro-Verbs 27:18-27 reveals:

- *He who tends the fig tree will eat its fruit*: When you guard the fig tree from the things that want to destroy it, you will have fruit in tact to eat. So, it is with the tree of your life. There are things out to destroy the tree so fruit will not come.
- *He who cares for his master will be honored*: To care for the needs of the master is of the highest honor and will be rewarded. The word *care* means to wait. When we wait on the Lord, we are honored with renewed strength.
- *As in water face reflects face so the heart of a man reflects man*: When you look into the mirror of the Word of God, who you are is reflected.
- *Sheol* (the nether world) *and Abaddon* (the place of perishing) *are never satisfied*: There is an insatiable drain of these two places.
- *The eyes of man are never satisfied*: The eyes of lust are insatiable

and lead to the nether world and the place of perishing.
- *The crucible is for silver and the furnace for gold*: The testing and purging of impurities.
- *A man is tested by the praise accorded him*: The fires will test and reveal the heart of a man.
- *Pound a fool in a mortar and pestle along with crushed grain, yet folly will not depart from him*: Gain crushed will separate the wheat from the chaff, but no amount of pounding will separate a fool from his folly.
- *Know well the condition of your flocks and pay attention to your herds*: Know well the condition of your body, soul and spirit. Pay attention to you and your walk with the Lord.
- *Riches are not forever nor does a crown endure to all generations*: Stuff is a fleeting thing.
- *When grass disappears, the new growth is seen*: Sometimes old things must leave so new things can come.
- *The herbs of the mountains are gathered in*: It is in our mountain top experience where we can gather the herbs as we go back into the valley
- *The lambs will be for your clothing*: The Lamb of God (Jesus) provided clothing of righteousness.
- *The goats will bring the price of a field*: The goats are not just for milk and food, but can also be used to negotiate a field.
- *There will be goats' milk enough for your food, for the food of your household and sustenance for your maidens*: Provision for you, your household, and maidens. If you treat your animal right and tend to your flocks and herds, you will always have food/provisions.

PRAYER: Lord, thank You for all You have given me in the natural and in the spiritual. I will keep my eyes and senses on the alert for my natural and my spiritual. Amen.

DAY 64
GIDDY UP

> *"Then Moses and the sons of Israel sang this song to the Lord, and said, 'I will sing to the Lord, for He is highly exalted; the horse and its rider He has hurled into the sea.'"*
>
> (Exodus 15:1)

Moses had gone into Egypt and delivered the children from the tyranny of the Pharaoh and brought them to the point of the Red Sea where they would cross over on dry land. But the Pharaoh had a change of heart and tried to recapture the children.

There was a sea on one side, blocking their escape, and on the other side horse, chariots, and an elite army drawing closer to recapture and put them back into slavery. They needed a miracle.

Moses stood poised, ready to flip the switch on the exit sign to show them the way. The Red Sea opened up and they went over dry land. The army pursued them on dry land until it became wet land, when the waters closed up and destroyed them.

> *"But the sons of Israel walked on dry land through the midst of the sea, and the waters were like a wall to them on their right hand and on their left. Thus the Lord saved Israel that day from the hands of the Egyptians, and Israel saw the Egyptians dead on the sea shore. And when Israel saw the great power which the*

Lord had used against the Egyptians, the people feared the Lord, and they believed in the Lord and in His servant Moses."
(Exodus 14:29-31)

Back in the 70's we would sing a chorus based on Exodus 15:1-2. As you can imagine, the chorus was a rowdy chorus of celebration from the domain of death and sin and deliverance.

The song was a declaration of the victory of the Lord over the horse and rider pursuing them through the Red Sea and how they [the horse and rider] were thrown into the sea. The song declared the Lord as their rock, strength, song, and their victory. The song ended with clapping and praising and exalting Him.

Once you sing that song through four or five times, you sense the victory. The song gets faster, the claps get louder, and the declarations of victory intensify. If that reaction happens with a few believers now, imagine how powerful that song would be right after the victory took place.

We need to learn to sing this song of victory before the deliverance or prayer is ever answered.

PRAYER: Lord, as the horses of the enemy bear down on me, thank You for the way of escape and protection for those enemies that are trying to recapture me. Amen.

DAY 65
THE WORTHY RECEIVING

"Worthy art Thou our Lord and our God, to receive glory and honor and power for Thou didst create all things, and because of Thy will they existed, and were created."

(Revelation 4:11)

WORTHY: Axios (ax'-ee-os**)**= *deserving, comparable* or *suitable* (as if *drawing* praise): - due reward, meet, [un-] worthy. (*Strong's*)

In our world, we have an award show for everything and everybody. People nominate and vote for movies, television shows, Broadway productions, music and musical artists, political experts, and anything or person that you can image that is deemed worthy of receiving an award.

What about God? Is He worthy of anything? According to the living creatures and twenty-four elders, God is worthy, deserving, suitable for praise and reward. *Strong's Concordance* defines what God is worthy for:

- Glory: (*glory* (as very *apparent*), in a wide application (literally or figuratively, objectively or subjectively): - dignity, glory (-ious), honour, praise, worship)
- Honor: a *value*, that is, *money* paid, or (concretely and collectively) *valuables*; by analogy *esteem* (especially of the highest degree), or the *dignity* itself: - honour, precious, price, some.
- Power: *force* (literally or figuratively); specifically miraculous

power (usually by implication a *miracle* itself): - ability, abundance, meaning, might (-ily, -y, -y deed), (worker of) miracle (-s), power, strength, violence, mighty (wonderful) work.

What makes the Lord so worthy of glory, honor, and power?

> "...*for Thou didst create all things, and because of Thy will they existed (were) and were created.*"
> (Revelation 4:11, addition mine)

Back in the 70's, we would sing this verse as we would praise and worship Him. The song we sang was taken from Revelation 4:11 and spoke of the worthiness of God and that He was worthy to receive glory, honor, and power. The reason being was that God created all things and, because of that, they existed. We would sing it directly to Him:

Lord you are worthy.

Some reading may know the tune and are singing along right now. For those who don't know the tune, I apologize; but you can read it and say it directly to the Lord.

What we are talking about is worship. We put a value on people and things and then we worship them. What value we put on them will determine how demonstrative we are toward them. We worship sports and sports heroes and go crazy at a game. We become very demonstrative towards them, until they fall from our grace and then we turn on them. What value do we put on God? Worship towards God is demonstrative also.

WORSHIP: proskuneo (pros-koo-neh'-o)= (meaning to *kiss*, like a dog *licking* his masters hand); to *fawn* or *crouch to*, that is, (literally or figuratively) *prostrate* oneself in homage (*do reverence to, adore*): - worship. (*Strong's*)

PRAYER: Lord, You and You alone, are worthy to receive my worship. I prostrate myself before You and listen for Your command to arise. When I hear Your voice in worship, I will rise up in obedience and truly worship with my actions. Amen.

DAY 66
LIVING PRAISE

"I will praise the Lord while I live; I will sing praises to my God while I have my being."

(Psalms 146:2)

Today, we begin with a series of Psalms that focuses on praising the Lord. From Psalm 146 to Psalm 150, the word *praise* is mentioned 44 times. One might wonder it if is okay to praise the Lord. It is not only okay, it is expected. In the words of Wayne Berry, the worship pastor where I attend church, when it says in Psalm 150, "let everything that hath breath praise the Lord..." Wayne's response is, "Are ya breathing?"

There are many words for the word *praise*. In this incident, the word is *halal*. Halal is not a quiet, reserved, non-demonstrative praise.

PRAISE: halal (haw-lal')=A primitive root; to *be clear* (originally of sound, but usually of color); to *shine*; hence to *make a show*, to *boast*; and thus to *be* (clamorously) *foolish*; to *rave*; causatively to *celebrate*; also to *stultify:* - (make) boast (self), celebrate, commend, (deal, make), fool (-ish, -ly), glory, give [light], be (make, feign self) mad (against), give in marriage, [sing, be worthy of] praise, rage, renowned, shine. (*Strong's*)

This is where we get the word *hallelujah* which means halal-Yaweh (Hallelu-jah). Halal praise in Psalm 146:6-10 means:

- **To be clear (of sound/color):** This is where there ain't no doubt that you are praising the Lord.
- **To shine:** This is not some dull, overcast, cloudy type of praise. There is a brightness to this type of praise.
- **To make a show:** The first thing I thought of was, "show and tell." The next thing I thought about was a performance for an audience of one (Him).
- **To boast:** Not bragging about me, but bragging about all the things that my God has done.
- **To be clamorously foolish:** When the Holy Spirit fell on the day of Pentecost, those who were on the outside looking in thought 120 people were drunk at 9:00 in the morning. There is going to be a ruckus when you begin to *Halal* the Lord.
- **To rave:** This means to talk wildly, as in delirium. In the words of the Buddy Holly song, rave on.
- **To celebrate:** We do not celebrate quietly. If you are at a football game, you do not celebrate quietly by sitting on your hands and muffling your voice. To have or participate in a party, drinking spree, or uninhibited good time is celebration.
- **To stultify:** to make, or cause to appear, foolish or ridiculous.

I like the idea of praising the Lord while I live. When I die, physically here on Earth my praises stop. You never go to a funeral or visitation of the dead and see the corpse *hallaling*. No, here on Earth we have to make a choice and then carry out that choice by actually praising the Lord. Physical death is merely a transition into His presence where the praises continues.

I view my earthly praises as practice for when I see Him face to face. At that time I will most likely fall on my face until He says, "Arise." So, for now, I will praise Him while I am breathing and have my mental ability.

Here are some reasons why the psalmist chose to praise the Lord. If you can't find a reason here, feel free to come up with your own reasons.

The Lord:

- Made Heaven and Earth
- Made the sea and all that is in them
- Keeps faith forever
- Executes justice for the oppressed
- Gives food to the hungry
- Sets the prisoners free
- Opens the eyes of the blind
- Raises up those who are bowed down
- Loves the righteous
- Protects the strangers
- Supports the fatherless and the widow
- Thwarts the way of the wicked
- Will reign forever

So, what are ya gonna do with all that? I believe I will *praise the Lord!*

PRAYER: Lord, You alone are worthy to be praise. Forgive me for when I grumble, complain, whine, grouch, grouse, kvetch (chronic grumbling) instead of getting my halal on. Amen.

DAY 67
CONCEALED WEAPONS OF MASS TRANSGRESSIONS

"He who conceals his transgressions will not prosper, but he who confesses and forsakes them will find compassion."
(Pro-Verbs 28:13)

TRANSGRESSION: Peshah (peh'-shah**)**=From H6586; a *revolt* (national, moral or religious): - rebellion, sin, transgression, trespassive **H6586: pasha' (**paw-shah'**)**=A primitive root (rather identical with H6585 through the idea of *expansion*); to *break* away (from just authority), that is, *trespass, apostatize, quarrel:* - offend, rebel, revolt, transgress (-ion, -or). (*Strong's*)

CONCEAL: kasah (kaw-saw'**)**=A primitive root; properly to *plump*, that is, *fill up* hollows; by implication to *cover* (for clothing or secrecy): - clad self, close, clothe, conceal, cover (self), (flee to) hide, overwhelm. (*Strong's*)

PROSPER: tsalach tsaleach (tsaw-lakh', tsaw-lay'-akh**)**=A primitive root; to *push* forward, in various senses (literally or figuratively, transitively or intransitively): - break out, come (mightily), go over, be good, be meet, be profitable, (cause to, effect, make to, send) prosper (-ity, -ous, -ously). (*Strong's*)

COMPASSIONS/MERCY: racham (raw-kham')=A primitive root; to *fondle*; by implication to *love*, especially to *compassionate:* - have compassion (on, upon), love, (find, have, obtain, shew) mercy (-iful, on, upon), (have) pity, Ruhamah, X surely. (*Strong's*)

I don't know about you, but I want to prosper. The alternative is to live in a mediocre type of way or below the poverty level. I want to prosper in His compassion for me. King David expressed a desire to be forgiven of his transgressions, sins, and iniquities in his psalms, including Psalms 32 and Psalms 51. David spoke of when he was silent about his transgressions/sins/iniquities.

> *"When I kept silent about my sin, my body wasted away through my groaning all day long. For day and night Thy hand was heavy upon me; my vitality was drained away as with the fever-heat of summer. [Selah] I acknowledged my sin to Thee, and my iniquity I did not hide; I said, I will confess my transgressions to the Lord, and Thou didst forgive me the guilt of my sin. [Selah]"*
> (Psalm 32:3-5)

There are two things that need to take place if you are going to enter into the prosperity and compassion of the Lord: (1) confess (2) forsake your transgressions.

CONFESS: yadah (yaw-daw')= literally to *use* (that is, hold out) *the hand*; physically to *throw* (a stone, an arrow) at or away; especially to *revere* or *worship* (with extended hands); intensively to *bemoan* (by wringing the hands): - cast (out), (make) confess (-ion), praise, shoot, (give) thank (-ful, -s, -sgiving). (*Strong's*)

I like that the idea of confessing is found in the same word for praise. Take your transgression and throw it like a stone to the Lord. When you do that, you are in essence praising and worshiping the Forgiver of your transgressions.

FORSAKE: 'azab (aw-zab')=A primitive root; to *loosen*, that is, *relinquish*, *permit*, etc.: - commit self, fail, forsake, fortify, help, leave (destitute, off), refuse, X surely. (*Strong's*)

As you confess your transgressions, they are loosened. You can begin to not do those things. That makes room for you to receive and be loosed from the guilt of that sin as David found out in Psalm 32.

> "... *I will confess my transgressions to the Lord'; and Thou didst forgive the guilt of my sin." [Selah]*
>
> (Psalm 32:5)

PRAYER: Thank You, Lord, for Your wonderful forgiveness, release from guilt, and Your wonderful prosperity and compassion. Amen.

DAY 68
THE CALLED MEETING

"Then the Lord called to Moses and spoke to him from the tent of meeting, saying..."

(Leviticus 1:1)

The children of Israel had been delivered from the bondage in Egypt and, a year later, they were still at the base of Mount Sinai. God's glory was present and they worshiped at the tabernacle in the wilderness.

The book of Leviticus is an instruction book for how to worship. The entire system of worship is based on the fact that the Lord is holy, and they should be holy.

"For I am the Lord your God...you shall be holy; for I am holy."

(Leviticus 11:44)

"Throughout the book of Leviticus there is continual instruction regarding dedication to personal holiness in response to the holiness of God. This emphasis is repeated over 50 times through the phrases, "I am the Lord" and I am holy." (*"The Bare Bones Bible Handbook"* by Jim George)

These wanderers were now called to be true sojourners, not just wandering aimlessly around, following their own lusts established in a pagan Egypt. They were following a holy God as they identified with His holiness and thus become holy. The called meeting by God, through Moses, was in order for Moses to speak to the sons of Israel and establish the practices of holiness in everything they did. These laws included areas of:

- Worship
- The Priesthood
- Uncleanness
- Acceptable Living

If these rules and regulations are followed, they would entire into a personal holiness as He is holy. I can't imagine doing these things today. No wonder they needed continual sacrifices because of their continual sins and continual failings. I constantly find myself needing forgiveness because of blowing the Ten Commandments. Thank God for Jesus the Christ…the Anointed One…the Messiah Who came and died on the cross in my place as the one and only sacrifice for my sins once and for all.

> *"For the love of Christ controls us, having concluded this, that One died for all therefore all died; and He died for all, that they who live should no longer live for themselves, but for Him who died and rose again on their behalf."*
>
> (2 Corinthians 5:14-15)

In the book of Hebrews, we see that there is a sacrifice, an offering that was made that was more powerful than any rule or regulations. It was longer lasting than any sacrifice, and was more potent than any blood of animal.

This sacrifice was the access key into the presence of God. No longer was a priest needed, because now they (and we) were(are) a priesthood of believers with a Great Priest (Jesus) over the household of God. Before they had no personal confidence to enter into His presence, and needed a priest to offer a sacrifice. Now *the sacrifice is the priest*, the Holy One, Jesus the Christ.

"Now where there is forgiveness of these things, there is no longer any offering for sin. Since therefore brethren we have confidence to enter the holy place by the blood of Jesus, by a new and living way which He inaugurated for us through the veil, that is, His flesh and since we have a great priest over the house of God, let us draw near with a sincere heart in full assurance of faith, having our hearts sprinkled clean from an evil conscience and our bodies washed with pure water."
(Hebrews 10:18-22)

When I was in Bible School, there was a poster hanging on the wall of our room. It talked about His sacrifice and the reason for His sacrifice, and that there was nothing we could do to bring anything to the table. It spoke of Jesus hanging on the cross.

JESUS HUNG UP FOR OUR HANGUPS

Now as He has been raised from the dead, we are called to service and worship. Because of His sacrifice of holiness, we are to offer ourselves to Him. The phrase, *"be holy because I am holy"* has not changed. What has changed is the fact that in our flesh we cannot do it; but by His mercies we can.

"I urge you therefore, brethren, by the mercies of God, to present your bodies a living and holy sacrifice, acceptable (well-pleasing) *to God, which is our spiritual service* (rational/reasonable) *of worship. And do not be conformed to this world, but be transformed by the renewing of your mind, that you may prove what the will of God is, that which is good and acceptable* (well-pleasing) *and perfect."*
(Romans 12:1, addition and emphasis mine)

PRAYER: Lord, I thank You for Your holy sacrifice that cleared the way for me to come into Your presence. I thank You that now I can offer You my good, acceptable, and perfect sacrifice by faith, and that it pleases You. Amen.

DAY 69
THE HAPPY ATTITUDE

"And opening His mouth He began to teach them, saying, 'Blessed are the...'"

(Matthew 5:2-3)

BLESSED: Makarios (mak-ar'-ee-os)=A prolonged form of the poetical μάκαρ makar (meaning the same); supremely *blest*; by extension *fortunate, well off:* - blessed, happy (X -ier). (*Strong's*)

Jesus is teaching about being happy in the Kingdom of God, and not just being happy and blessed, but supremely blest and well off. Now that is what I want in my life.

But the key to this happy blessing is found in the attitude. I love saying that *the beatitudes—be the attitude*—that I need to *be having*. In other words, for the blessings to come, there needs to be an *attitudinal adjustment* in my kingdom thinking. In Matthew 5:3-12, we see who is supremely blessed and happy:

BLESSED/SUPREMELY BLEST/HAPPY ARE:

- *The poor in spirit: Theirs is the kingdom of Heaven*
- *Those who mourn: For they shall be comforted*
- *The gentle: For they shall inherit the earth*
- *Those who hunger and thirst for righteousness: They shall be satisfied*

- *The merciful: For they shall receive mercy*
- *The pure in heart: They shall see God*
- *The peacemakers: They shall be called sons of God*
- *Those who have been persecuted for the sake of righteousness: Theirs is the kingdom of Heaven*
- *When men revile you and persecute you and say all kinds of evil against you falsely on account of Me: Rejoice and be glad for your reward in heaven is great*

The blessings seem to come in the face of hard times. The blessings come when you adopt a positive attitude (Be Attitude) with a positive cause-and-effect. There are two things that follow up the beatitudes in the face of the negative.

REJOICE: chairo (khah'ee-ro)=A primary verb; to be full of *cheer*, that is, calmly *happy* or well off; impersonal especially as a salutation (on meeting or parting), *be well:* - farewell, be glad, God speed, greeting, hail, joy (-fully), rejoice. (*Strong's*)

BE EXCEEDING GLAD: agalliao (ag-al-lee-ah'-o)=From αγαν agan (*much*) and G242; properly to *jump for joy*, that is, *exult:* - be (exceeding) glad, with exceeding joy, rejoice (greatly). (*Strong's*)

In the face of the negative, the response is not to gripe, grumble, complain, grouse, mumble, mutter, whine, and kvetch (the *k* is silent). When you walk by faith and not by sight in the face of the negative, you should:

- Be full of cheer
- Be calmly happy
- Be well off
- Be well
- Be glad
- Be full of joy
- Rejoice greatly

- Jump for hoy
- Exult

Now, that is an Attitudinal Adjustment.

PRAYER: Lord, thank You for the blessing of being happy in You. Amen.

DAY 70
PRAISE TIME FOUR

"Praise (halal) the Lord! For it is good to sing praises (zamar) to our God; for it is pleasant and praise (tehhillah) is becoming."
(Psalm 147:1, addition mine)

This wonderful *praise psalm* deals specifically with Jerusalem's restoration and prosperity.

As with many of the Psalms that have a historical perspective, I tend to apply them to my every day nitty-gritty, real life situations and circumstances. I once was broken, but Jesus came to die on the cross; to be buried; and to be raised from the dead. I believed with my heart that God raised Him from the dead. With my mouth I confessed that Jesus is Lord. I became a new creation who was restored and made prosperous in my spirit.

In Psalm 147, the psalmist uses four types of praise to describe the joy of restoration and prosperity. In the first verse of Psalm 147, there are three different words for *praise*. The word *praise* occurs seven times with four different meanings. This is not the first psalm that interweaves different words for *praise*, but I find it interesting that, in the very first sentence, there are three words for *praise* and later another word for *praise*. You get the idea that the psalmist wants to *praise the Lord* times four.

PRAISE: halal (haw-lal')=A primitive root; to *be clear* (originally of sound, but usually of color); to *shine*; hence to *make a show*; to *boast*; and thus to *be* (clamorously) *foolish*; to *rave*; causatively to *celebrate*; also to *stultify*: - (make) boast (self), celebrate, commend, (deal, make), fool (-ish, -ly), glory, give [light], be (make, feign self) mad (against), give in marriage, [sing, be worthy of] praise, rage, renowned, shine. (*Strong's*)

PRAISE: zamar (zaw-mar')=A primitive root (perhaps identical with H2168 through the idea of *striking* with the fingers); properly to *touch* the strings or parts of a musical instrument, that is, *play* upon it; to make *music*, accompanied by the voice; hence to *celebrate* in song and music: - give praise, sing forth praises, psalms. (*Strong's*)

PRAISE: tehillah (teh-hil-law')=From H1984; *laudation*; specifically (concretely) a *hymn*: - praise. **H1984: halal** (haw-lal')=A primitive root; to *be clear* (originally of sound, but usually of color); to *shine*; hence to *make a show*, to *boast*; and thus to *be* (clamorously) *foolish*; to *rave*; causatively to *celebrate*; also to *stultify*: - (make) boast (self), celebrate, commend, (deal, make), fool (-ish, -ly), glory, give [light], be (make, feign self) mad (against), give in marriage, [sing, be worthy of] praise, rage, renowned, shine. (*Strong's*)

PRAISE: shabach (shaw-bakh')=A primitive root; properly to *address* in a loud tone, that is, (specifically) *loud*; figuratively to *pacify* (as if by words): - commend, glory, keep in, praise, still, triumph. (*Strong's*)

It is good, pleasant and becoming to praise the Lord. Do you need a reason to praise the Lord? It is always proper to give our God praise. Here are some reasons that the psalmist lists in reference to Jerusalem's restoration and prosperity, and I can join in with the choir in reference to my restoration and prosperity in Christ.

- The Lord builds up Jerusalem.
- He gathers the outcasts of Israel.
- He heals the brokenhearted.

- He binds up their wounds.
- He counts the number of the stars and He gives names to all of them.
- He supports the afflicted.
- He brings down the wicked to the ground.
- He covers the heavens with clouds.
- He provides rain for the earth.
- He makes grass to grow on the mountains.
- He gives to the beast and young ravens which cry.
- He has strengthened the bars of your gates.
- He has blessed your sons within you.
- He makes peace in your borders.
- He satisfies you with the finest wheat.
- He sends forth His command to the earth.
- His word runs very swiftly.
- He gives snow like wool.
- He scatters the hoarfrost like ashes.
- He casts forth His ice as fragments.
- He sends for His word and melts them.
- He causes His wind to blow and the waters to flow.
- He declares His words to Jacob.
- He declares His statues and His ordinances to Israel.

I am beginning to see why one form of praise is not enough to praise the Lord for all He has done for Jerusalem or for me.

PRAYER: All I can say is: (1) Lord is Praise the Lord; (2) Praise the Lord; (3) Praise the Lord; (4) Praise the Lord…and the beat (praise) goes on. Four praises Lord, are only the beginning for how grateful I am to You. Amen.

DAY 71
THE RIGHTEOUS CONCERNS

> *"The righteous are concerned for the rights of the poor, the wicked does not understand such concern."*
>
> (Pro-Verbs 29:7)

I believe that it safe to say that the Lord is concerned for the poor in the physical and in the spirit. This first thing Jesus said when He opened His mouth and began to teach them (Matthew 5:2) was to pronounce a blessing of being supremely blest and happy.

> *"Blessed are the poor in spirit, for theirs is the kingdom of heaven."*
>
> (Matthew 5:3)

> *"...blessed are you who are poor, for yours is the kingdom of God."*
>
> (Luke 6:20)

When Jesus was freshly anointed by the Father with the Holy Spirit, one of His first teachings occurred when He went to the synagogue. He took the book of the prophet Isaiah and read:

> *"The Spirit of the Lord is upon Me, because He anointed Me to preach the gospel to the poor..."*
>
> (Luke 4:18)

POOR: Dal (dal)=From H1809; properly *dangling*, that is, (by implication) *weak* or *thin:* - lean, needy, poor (man), weaker. **H1809: dalal** (daw-lal')=A primitive root (compare H1802); to *slacken* or *be feeble*; figuratively to *be oppressed:* - bring low, dry up, be emptied, be not equal, fail, be impoverished, be made thin. (*Strong's*)

POOR: ptochos (pto-khos')=From πτώσσω ptōssō (to *crouch*; akin to G4422 and the alternate of G4098); a *beggar* (as *cringing*), that is, *pauper* (strictly denoting absolute or public *mendicancy*, although also used in a qualified or relative sense; whereas G3993 properly means only *straitened* circumstances in private), literally (often as noun) or figuratively (*distressed*): - beggar (-ly), poor. (*Strong's*)

We often think of being poor as being financially depleted, and being without food, clothes or home. This is surely part of being poor, however there is a spiritual quality to someone being poor. I think that is why we have the pictures of being poor and being poor in spirit. When we see the definition, it brings clarity to the word "poor."

- Dangling
- Weak or thin
- Lean
- Needy
- Slacken
- Feeble
- Oppressed
- Bring low
- Dry up
- Be emptied
- Be not equal
- Fail be impoverished
- Be made thin

I know for a fact that someone can have all of these things in their lives and have a bank account that is overflowing.

When I worked for a home health company in Nashville Tennessee, I had to go to "the projects" to see a patient. The area was known as "little Vietnam" because of the gang wars at night. If you went in the mornings, the gang members were usually asleep or drunk, so there was not much activity. Everywhere there was a stench of vomit and general filth.

I knocked on the door of the patient whom I was there to see. The door opened and I was greeted by a woman who invited me in and praised God that I was there. Inside was the cleanest apartment I have ever been; it was spotless, it smelled good, and there were no cockroaches.

This woman was poor, living in poverty, but she did not allow the poverty in her life. She told me that God was going to deliver her out of the projects, but until then, she would live for Him. I came back the following week and she was not there. I eventually found her in a new place. When she opened door, she said, "Praise God, didn't I tell you that He would deliver me?"

You may not be rich but you don't have to be poor. I have been to some of the poorest places around the world, in Mexico, Peru, Africa, Guatemala, but the people I met there have been rich in the spirit because the words of Jesus were true; theirs was the kingdom of Heaven, on Earth as it is in Heaven. (Matthew 5:3; Matthew 6:10)

PRAYER: Lord, show me how to be rich in You. Amen.

DAY 72
KVETCHING 101

"And all the sons of Israel grumbled against Moses and Aaron; and the whole congregation said to them, 'Would that we would that we had died in the land of Egypt! Or would that we had died in this wilderness.'"

(Numbers 14:2)

GRUMBLED/MURMURED: lun lıyn (loon, leen)=A primitive root; to *stop* (usually over night); by implication to *stay* permanently; hence (in a bad sense) to be *obstinate* (especially in words, to *complain*): - abide (all night), continue, dwell, endure, grudge, be left, lie all night, (cause to) lodge (all night, in, -ing, this night), (make to) murmur, remain, tarry (all night, that night). (*Strong's*)

Don't you just love to hear someone complain about something or someone? Doesn't it just build you up in your spirit and make you want to keep on keeping on in your quest?

Some of the words for this thing called *grumbling* would include:

- Grumbling
- Murmuring
- Griping
- Complaining
- Whining

- Grousing
- Kvetching

The last one is a Hebrew word that, for me, is the best one. It is pronounced "vetching," with a silent *k* and it means "to complain," especially chronically, while the noun means, "kvetcher, a person who kvetches."

The sons of Israel had just heard a report from 12 spies about what they had seen in the Promised Land. There were reports of large fruit, milk and honey flowing. Then they said the word, "nevertheless," which meant that there was good but there was also bad. They reported of strong people, of large and fortified cities. Then they dropped the other shoe with the word, "moreover" which meant not only was there strong people, large and fortified cities, but there were descendants of Anak, Amelek, and all the "-ites," including Hittites, Jebusites, Amorites, and the Canaanites.

In Numbers 13:30, we see the response of the bad report was such that Caleb, *"quieted the people"* with the positive report. I can imagine the noise level that needed to be quieted was *not* positive noise, but the beginning of the grumbling. Caleb said, "We should *by all means go up* and *take possession* of it (the land), for *we shall surely overcome it* (the land)." [emphasis and addition mine] The other spies continued with their kvetching bad report in Numbers 13:31-33.

- We are *not able*
- They are *too strong*
- The land *devours* its inhabitants
- All the men we saw are of *great size*
- There saw the *Nephilim* (the sons of Anak)

NOTE: The *Nephilim* (plural) are the offspring of the "sons of God" and the "daughters of men" mentioned in Genesis 6:4, or giants who inhabit Canaan in Numbers 13:33. A similar word with different vowel-sounds is used in Ezekiel 32:27 to refer to dead Philistine warriors. (Wikipedia)

- We became *like grasshoppers* in *our own sight*
- So, *we were* in *their sight*

When all was said and done from both sides—with Joshua and Caleb with a positive report, and the other ten with a negative report—the people had to choose who they were going to believe and how they were going to react (in the flesh) and respond (in the Spirit). We are faced with these types of choices all the time. What we choose is manifested in our voice with either grumbling or praise.

> *"Then (after the good and bad reports) the congregation lifted up their voices and cried, and then the people wept that night."*
> (Numbers 14:1, addition mine)

The people had the night to sleep on it. The next day they chose, which was to grumble against Moses and Aaron, with their grumbling, murmuring, griping, complaining, whining, grousing, and yes, my favorite word, kvetching (to complain, especially chronically).

In Numbers 14:2-4, we see that all the sons of Israel and the whole congregation began to grumble against Moses and Aaron by saying:

- Would that we had died in the land of Egypt!
- Would that we had died in this wilderness!
- Why is the Lord bringing us into this land to fall by the sword?
- Our wives and our little ones will become plunder.
- Would it not be better for us to return to Egypt?
- Let us appoint a leader and return to Egypt.

I know from personal experience that when I grumble and complain with the bad reports of our times, I begin to follow the pattern of the grumblers and kvetchers. I begin to long for my life before I was

Christian or at least to die on my journey and go to Heaven instead of facing the pre-promised land troubles. I begin to question the Lord's motives in my life as doubt and fear comes in like a serpent in a garden where he (the serpent) whispers, "Did God really say?" Then I try to find other leaders to help me return to my old ways.

PRAYER: Lord, forgive me for believing bad reports on my journey. Forgive me Lord, for choosing grumbling, murmuring, griping, complaining, whining, grousing, kvetching (to complain, especially chronically) and not choosing praising You. Amen.

DAY 73
THE GREAT GO-MISSION AGAIN

> *"And He said to them, 'Go into all the world, and preach the gospel to all creation.'"*
>
> (Mark 16:15)

Jesus the Christ (the Messiah), who was God in the flesh, came to planet Earth in the form of a little baby, in a little country (Israel), in a little town (Bethlehem), in a little manger. In reality Jesus was the first missionary who left His country (Heaven) to go the mission field of Earth.

He came for a purpose that He demonstrated for three years.

> *"...The son of God appeared for this purpose, that He (Jesus) might destroy the works of the d-evil (the evil one)."*
>
> (1 John 3:8, addition mine)

> *"The Spirit of the Lord is upon Me, because He anointed Me to preach the gospel to the poor. He has sent Me to proclaim release to the captives, and the recovery of sight to the blind, to set free those who are downtrodden, to proclaim the favorable year of the Lord."*
>
> (Luke 4:18-19)

> *"You know of Jesus of Nazareth, how God anointed Him with the Holy Spirit and with power, and how He went about doing*

> *good and healing all who were oppressed by the d-evil; for God was with Him."*
>
> (Acts 10:38)

Jesus went about for three years demonstrating what He taught His disciples to pray with:

> *"Thy kingdom Thy will be done on earth as it is in heaven."*
>
> (Matthew 6:10)

The Great Go-Mission was for Jesus' disciples to continue with what He started. He spoke of this continuation of His mission as He spoke to His followers about His soon departure.

> *"Believe Me that I am in the Father, and the Father in Me; otherwise believe on account of the works themselves. Truly, truly, I say to you, he who believes in Me, the works that I do shall he do also; and greater works than these shall he do; because I go to the Father, and whatever you ask (in reference to the greater works) in My name (the authority), that I will do, that the Father may be glorified in the Son."*
>
> (John 14:11-13, addition mine)

The Great Go-Mission found in Matthew, Mark, Luke, John, Acts is:

- *"Go therefore and make disciples of all the nations, baptizing them in the name of the Father and the Son and the Holy Spirit, teaching them to observe all that I commanded you; and lo, I am with you always, even to the end of the age."* (Matthew 28:19-20)
- *"And He said to them, 'Go into all the world and preach the gospel to all creation.'"* (Mark 15:15)
- *"Then He opened their minds to understand the Scriptures, and He said to them, 'Thus it is written, that the Christ should suffer and rise again from the dead the third day; and that repentance for forgiveness of sins should*

> be proclaimed in His name to all the nations, beginning from Jerusalem. You are witnesses of these things. And behold, I am sending forth the promise of My Father upon you; but you are to stay in the city until you are clothed with power form on high.'" (Luke 24:45-49)

- *"Jesus therefore said to them again, 'Peace be with you; as the Father has sent Me, I also send you.' And when He had said this, He breathed on them, and said to them, 'Receive the Holy Spirit. If you forgive the sins of any, their sins have been forgiven them; if you retain the sins of any, they have been retained.'" (John 20:21-23)*
- *"But you shall receive power when the Holy Spirit has come upon you; and You shall be My witnesses both in Jerusalem, and in all Judea and Samaria, and even to the remotest part of the earth." (Acts 1:8)*

When we hear the word, *mission* we think of going across the waters to a foreign land. That is true sometimes, but in the case of Jesus' disciples, for the most part they did not cross the waters. They started in Jerusalem where they lived and then branched out. We can start out being a witness where we are in our home, at our workplace, out into the marketplace, and beyond. It is not called The Great *Stay*-mission but The Great *Go*-mission.

PRAYER: Father, I listen for Your voice not to tell me to go, but to tell me where and when. You speak and I will obey. Amen.

DAY 74
RAISE SOME HALAL

"Praise the Lord…!"

(Psalm 148:1)

We continue on with the "praise psalms" at the end of the book of Psalms. In Psalm 148, the word *praise* appears 13 times in 14 verses. Again, we see that the psalmist feels that we need to get our praise on. In Psalm 147, there were four words for the word *praise* but here in Psalm 148, with our 13 words of praise there is only one word. The word is *halal*.

PRAISE: halal (haw-lal')=A primitive root; to *be clear* (originally of sound, but usually of color); to *shine*; hence to *make a show*; to *boast*; and thus to *be* (clamorously) *foolish*; to *rave*; causatively to *celebrate*; also to *stultify*: - (make) boast (self), celebrate, commend, (deal, make), fool (-ish, -ly), glory, give [light], be (make, feign self) mad (against), give in marriage, [sing, be worthy of] praise, rage, renowned, shine. (*Strong's*)

In previous devotions, we explained what this word *halal* means, and it is definitely rowdy. I have likened this praise like booster rockets breaking free from the gravitational pull of Earth. When we are pulled down by this world with all the problems, we need something to break the spiritual gravitational pull of Earth and that is the booster rocket of praise.

In Psalm 148, the psalmist invokes the whole creations to *halal the Lord*.

- Praise the Lord.
- Praise the Lord from the heavens.
- Praise Him in the heights.
- Praise Him, all His angels.
- Praise Him, all His hosts.
- Praise Him, sun and moon.
- Praise Him, all stars of light.
- Praise Him, highest heavens.
- Praise Him, the waters that are above the heavens.

The psalmist says that we are to let/allow the praise of the name of the Lord to flow. Why? Because He commanded and they were created. He established them forever and ever. He has made a decree which will not pass away.

- Praise the Lord from the earth including
- Sea monsters and all deeps
- Fire and hail
- Snow and clouds
- Stormy wind
- Mountains and hills
- Fruit trees and all cedars
- Beasts and all cattle
- Creeping things
- Winged fowl
- Kings of the earth
- All peoples
- Princes
- All judges of the earth
- Both young men and virgins
- Old men and children

You can add to the list because there is nothing under the sun that does not need to get their halal on.

PRAYER: Father, I just want to be clear, to shine, to make a show, to boast, to be clamorously foolish, to rave, and to celebrate... *You, Lord!* Amen.

DAY 75

THE TESTED WORD

"Every word of God is tested; He is a shield to those who take refuge in Him."

(Pro-Verbs 30:5)

TESTED: tsaraph (tsaw-raf')=A primitive root; to *fuse* (metal), that is, *refine* (literally or figuratively): - cast, (re-) fine (-er), founder, goldsmith, melt, pure, purge away, try. (*Strong's*)

A *word* is a thought that is expressed either by speaking it, writing it, drawing it, or signing it.

God's thoughts are His will in a matter. We see that in the beginning, God had a thought about the world. What you could see was darkness, a formless void, and God spoke His will by saying:

"Let there be light."

(Genesis 1:3)

The cause-and-effect of God speaking His mind was:

"...and there was light."

(Genesis 1:3)

God saw His thought come into existence by His Word and He said that it:

"...was good."
(Genesis 1:4)

His Word is tried and tested and proven to be true and pure.

It is so very important when we are facing darkness, formless and void things in our lives. that we renew our minds with the Word of God. That we let/allow our minds to dwell on the Word of God. That we speak the Word of God and that we let/allow our actions to be based on the Word of God and not what we feel or see. We need to restrain our thoughts, words, and deeds based not on our thinking, but on His thinking.

> *"Unrestrained thoughts (what we think) produces unrestrained words (what we say) resulting in unrestrained actions (what we do)."*
> (Unknown, but I have quoted it so many times I think I came up with it.)

The Word of God is tested. The Word of God is tried and proven to be effective and able to stand under times of stress. We know that our faith comes by hearing and hearing by the Word of Christ. (Romans 10:17) When that faith comes, we are able to believe and hope in the face of the unseen or things not revealed to our senses. When we can't see something, we must have faith towards, and in, God and Jesus. So, the Word of God is tested and now it is time to "test ourselves."

> *"Test yourselves to see if you are in the faith; examine yourselves! Or do you not recognize this about yourselves that Jesus Christ is in you—unless indeed you fail the test? But I trust that you will realize that we ourselves do not fail the test."*
> (2 Corinthians 13:5-6)

> *"...discipline yourself for the purpose of godliness."*
> 1 Timothy 4:7)

> *"But solid food is for the mature who, because of practice have their senses trained to discern good and evil."*
>
> (Hebrews 5:14)

DISCIPLINE/EXERCISE: gumnazo (goom-nad'-zo)=From G1131; to *practise naked* (in the games), that is, *train* (figuratively): - exercise. G1131: gumnos (*goom-nos'*)=Of uncertain affinity; *nude* (absolutely or relatively, literally or figuratively): - naked. (*Strong's*)

The idea of this self-discipline and habitual exercise is to do it unencumbered of the things that will trip you up.

BY REASON OF USE: Hexis (hex'-is)=*habit*, that is, (by implication) *practice:* - use. (*Strong's*)

> *"Therefore, since we have so great a cloud of witnesses surrounding us, let us also lay aside every encumbrance, and the sin which so easily entangles us, and let us run with endurance the race that is set before us."*
>
> (Hebrews 12:1)

When we begin to discipline, exercise, habitually allow the Word to work in us, we are in essence testing the Word in us. As His Word is found to be pure, it becomes a shield to us as we take refuge in Him.

PRAYER: Lord, thank You for sanctifying me in truth, and as You said in Your prayer to the Father, *"Thy Word is truth."* Thank You that the Father's word is tried and tested in my life. Amen.

DAY 76
THE TEN WORDS

"I am the Lord your God, Who brought you out of the land of Egypt, out of the house of slavery."

(Deuteronomy 5:6)

People tend to think of the Ten Commandments as the things that you have to do to get to Heaven, to be a Christian, the lifestyle needed to stay on the straight and narrow. I had a friend that told me once that he tried to keep the Commandments, but sometimes he missed the mark and kept 6 of the 10.

James was pretty clear on what happens if you missed one of the Commandments and the guilt factor.

"For whoever keeps the whole law and yet stumbles in one point, he has become guilty of all. For He who said, 'Do not commit adultery' also said, 'Do not commit murder.' Now if you do not commit adultery, but do commit murder, you have become a transgressor of the law."

(James 2:10-11)

Jesus often spoke about the Commandments.

"You have heard that it was said, 'You shall not commit adultery;' but I say to you, that everyone who looks on a woman to lust for

> *her has committed adultery with her already in his heart."*
> (Matthew 5:27-28)

The Ten Commandments are also known at The Decalogue, which is also known as The Ten Words. It is like The Ten Words are the main points of the Law, but the following chapters in Deuteronomy outlines and expands what they mean. It is like a policy and procedure handbook, where the Ten Commands are the policy and the following books explain how to carry out the procedures.

They were given to Moses on Mount Sinai as recorded in Exodus 20:2-17, and then recounted again in the Deuteronomy 5:6-21. Even though the children were brought out of the land of Egypt—which was also known as the house of slavery—they were free, but still subject to law. Sometimes we tend to think that we are free, but as Paul wrote to the Galatians:

> *"It was for freedom that Christ set us free; therefore, keep standing firm and do not be subject again to a yoke of slavery."*
> (Galatians 5:1)

Ben Kinchlow, the former co-host of *The 700 Club,* wrote a book called "You Don't Have To If You Don't Want To (The Marvelous Power to Choose)." In the book, he speaks of the laws that we have been given and how they can be violated by our power of choice. He gives an example of traffic laws that have been laid out for our safety. We have roads with lines in the middle of the road. One car stays on one side and the other car stays on the other side. As long as we adhere to the lines, traffic will flow smoothly; but when we choose not to do what we are supposed to do, then we may have an accident. The cause-and-effect of disobedience can be devastating.

So, it is with these laws that God gave Moses and the children of Israel for their journey in the wilderness. The laws were not given to bring the children back into slavery, but given so they could be free.

> *"For you were called to freedom, brethren only do not turn your freedom into an opportunity for the flesh but through love serve one another."*
>
> (Galatians 5:13)

Although Christ has fulfilled the Law, it does not mean that The Ten Commandments are antiquated rules and regulations that would not be beneficial for us today. Here are The Ten Words (Decalogue) that are commandments and not suggestions. And God spoke all these words, saying,

> *"I am the Lord thy God, which have brought thee out of the land of Egypt, out of the house of bondage.*
> *Thou shalt have no other gods before me.*
> *Thou shalt not make unto thee any graven image, or any likeness of anything that is in Heaven above, or that is in the earth beneath, or that is in the water under the earth. Thou shalt not bow down thyself to them, nor serve them: for I the Lord thy God am a jealous God, visiting the iniquity of the fathers upon the children unto the third and fourth generation of them that hate me; And shewing mercy unto thousands of them that love me, and keep my commandments.*
> *Thou shalt not take the name of the Lord thy God in vain; for the Lord will not hold him guiltless that taketh his name in vain. Remember the Sabbath day, to keep it holy. Six days shalt thou labor, and do all thy work: But the seventh day is the Sabbath of the Lord thy God: in it thou shalt not do any work, thou, nor thy son, nor thy daughter, thy manservant, nor thy maidservant, nor thy cattle, nor thy stranger that is within thy gates: For in six days the Lord made Heaven and Earth, the sea, and all that in them is, and rested the seventh day: wherefore the Lord blessed the Sabbath day, and hallowed it.*

Honor thy father and thy mother: that thy days may be long upon the land which the Lord thy God giveth thee.
Thou shalt not kill.
Thou shalt not commit adultery.
Thou shalt not steal.
Thou shalt not bear false witness against thy neighbor.
Thou shalt not covet thy neighbor's house. Thou shalt not covet thy neighbor's wife, or his manservant, nor his maidservant, or his ox, nor his ass, or anything that is thy neighbor's."

In this day and age, there are certain people who do not want to be reminded of these 10 words, because they feel that a God that they really don't believe in is trying to keep them in slavery. After all, in their minds, freedom means doing anything that they want to do anytime with anyone. These commands are just too restricting for them.

PRAYER: Father, I know that there is nothing I can do to earn, win, and deserve my freedom; but Lord help me to obey and keep Your commands. Lord, out of the hundreds and hundreds of commandments, thank You for distilling them down to loving You, loving myself, and loving my neighbor as myself. Amen.

DAY 77
THE RULE OF GOLD

"And just as you want men to treat you, treat them in the same way."

(Luke 6:31)

"Therefore, whatever you want others to do for you do so for them, for this is the Law and the Prophets."

(Matthew 7:12)

"Remember the Golden Rule...He who has the gold, rules."
("The Wizard of Id")

The Golden Rule is found throughout history and, in some form or fashion, within many religions. But Jesus epitomized the rule within His teachings and pointed to the Law and the Prophets for the foundation of the rule of gold. This rule just makes common sense in a senseless world.

As we look back to the Law and the Prophets, we see two areas as foundational for the *"do unto others as you would have them do unto you."* It is the ultimate sowing and reaping, seedtime and harvest, cause-and-effect of reciprocity.

First, look at the main statement of faith for the Jew called the *Shema*:

"Hear, O Israel! The Lord is our God, the Lord is one! And you

> *shall love the Lord your God with all your heart and with all your soul and with all your might."*
>
> (Deuteronomy 6:4-5)

> *"You shall not take vengeance, nor bear any grudge against the sons of your people, but you shall love your neighbor as yourself; I am the Lord."*
>
> (Leviticus 19:18)

In the Old Testament, there are approximately 613 laws, but according to Jesus—when He was quizzed by one of the scribes (one who counted the laws)—who asked Jesus which one was the foremost (first of all) of all the Laws. Jesus' response points to the Golden Rule of the Old Testament.

> *"Jesus answered, 'The foremost is "Hear, O Israel; the Lord our God is one Lord (Deuteronomy 6:4) and you shall love the Lord your God with all your heart, and with all your soul, and with all your mind, and with all your strength." (Deuteronomy 6:5) The second is this," you shall love your neighbor as yourself." (Leviticus 19:18) There is no other commandment greater than these."'*
>
> (Mark 12:28-31; Matthew 22:36-40; Luke 10:25-28, addition mine)

It is said that, in the book of James, that there is a "royal law." When you fulfil this law you are, *"doing well."*

> *"If, however, you are fulfilling the royal law* (of our King), *according to the Scripture, you shall love your neighbor as yourself, you are* doing well.*"*
>
> (James 2:8, addition and emphasis mine)

In the Luke passage, when Jesus said to love your neighbor as yourself, the lawyer tried to cover himself by asking clarification of just who this neighbor is.

> *"But wishing to justify himself (the lawyer), he said to Jesus, 'And who is my neighbor?'"*
> (Luke 10:29, addition mine)

Jesus answered him with a parable of the Good Samaritan. (Luke 10:30-37) The parable is:

- A certain man going down from Jerusalem to Jericho.
- He fell among robbers who stripped him and beat him and went off leaving him half dead.
- A priest passed by going down the road, saw him, and passed on by on the other side.
- A Levite also saw him and passed by on the other side.
- A certain Samaritan (who was considered unclean to the point that the *religious* Jews would not even enter their country, but bypass the region of Samaria) was on a journey. He saw him, and he felt compassion. He came to him, bandaged his wounds, pouring on oil and wine on the wounds, put him on his own beast, and brought him to an in, and took care of him.
- On the next day, he took out two denarii (a day's wage), gave them to the innkeeper, instructed him to take care of the man, and then told him that whatever he spend for this man's care, he (the Samaritan) would repay him on his return trip.

Jesus then asked which of these three people, did the lawyer think proved to be a "neighbor" to the man who had fallen into the hands of the robbers.

> *"And he (the lawyer) said, 'The one who showed mercy toward him.' And Jesus said to him, 'Go and do the same thing.'"*
> (Luke 10:37, addition mine)

The Golden Rule springs from the love for the Father, which is expressed in the love you have for yourself as you do unto others as the Lord has done unto you. Expressed in mercy, The Golden Rule comes out of a Golden Heart.

PRAYER: Lord, help me treat others in the spirit of the Samaritan who epitomizes The Golden Rule. Amen.

DAY 78
THE LET/ALLOW INVOCATION

"Praise the Lord! Sing a new song and His praise in the congregation of the godly ones."

(Psalm 149:1)

The subtitle in my Bible for Psalms 149 is, "Israel Invoked to Praise the Lord."

Sometimes, we need encouragement to do certain things in our lives. That includes singing songs to the Lord and praising Him. You would think that it would come naturally; but we are humans who, at times, put our minds on automatic pilot and just float through life not thinking, even in our spiritual lives. That's why we really do need each other to give each other a little nudge to do the things that we know that we need to be doing. The psalmist is asking for help to praise and sing to the Lord.

PRAISE: halal (haw-lal')=A primitive root; to *be clear* (originally of sound, but usually of color); to *shine*; hence to *make a show*; to *boast*; and thus to *be* (clamorously) *foolish*; to *rave*; causatively to *celebrate*; also to *stultify*: - (make) boast (self), celebrate, commend, (deal, make), fool (-ish, -ly), glory, give [light], be (make, feign self) mad (against), give in marriage, [sing, be worthy of] praise, rage, renowned, shine. (*Strong's*)

SING: shıyr shur (sheer, shoor)= through the idea of *strolling* minstrelsy); to *sing*: - behold sing (-er, -ing man, -ing woman). (*Strong's*)

Again, this praising is not just a quiet and passive praise, but a rowdy version. And the song that we are to sing is not the same, old, habitual, mundane song, stale song ...but a brand fresh song.

NEW: chadash (khaw-dawsh')=From H2318; *new:* - fresh, new thing.
H2318: chadash (khaw-dash')=A primitive root; to *be new*, causatively to *rebuild:* - renew, repair. (*Strong's*)

As the psalmist is encouraging praise and fresh songs to be sung, he is speaking to the congregation of the godly ones. That would include you and me. There are seven "lets" listed in this psalm of praise and singing of new songs. I like that word *let*, because it speaks of someone who has control and letting something happen by choice. According to Dictionary.com, the word *let* means, *to allow or permit*. Let us see what the psalmist is encouraging the congregation of the godly ones to allow or permit.

- Let (allow/permit) Israel be glad in His Maker
- Let (allow/permit) the sons of Zion rejoice in their King
- Let (allow/permit) them praise with dancing
- Let (allow/permit) them sing praises to Him with timbral and lyre

Why? Because the Lord takes pleasure in His people, and He will beautify the afflicted ones with salvation.

- Let (allow/permit) the godly ones exult (to *jump* for joy, that is, *exult:* - be joyful, rejoice, triumph) in glory
- Let (allow/permit) them sing for joy on their beds
- Let (allow/permit) the high praises of God be in their mouth, and a two-edged sword in their hand.

These things that the psalmist wants the congregation of the godly ones to let/allow/permit is for authority over their enemies.

- To execute vengeance on the nations
- To execute punishment on the peoples
- To bind their kings with chains
- To bind their nobles with fetters of iron
- To execute on them the judgment written

Now this is for those people in that time-space continuum, but I think that when we praise the Lord (to *be clear* (originally of sound, but usually of color); to *shine*; hence to *make a show*, to *boast*; and thus to *be* (clamorously) *foolish*; to *rave*; causatively to *celebrate*; also to *stultify*) and when we sing a new and fresh song (*strolling* minstrelsy) and we exult (be joyful, rejoice, triumph) in glory), it is an honor to do so.

> "...*this is an honor for all His godly ones.* Praise the Lord (Hallelujah/Halal to Yawheh)."
> (Psalm 149:9, addition and emphasis mine)

PRAYER: Lord, I will be demonstrative in my praise and singing to You. What an honor! Amen.

DAY 79
THE EXCELLENT WIFE (My Wife)

"An excellent wife who can find (who can find an excellent wife)? For her worth is far above jewels."
(Pro-Verbs 31:10, addition mine)

I approach this devotion very carefully. For many years, whenever I heard someone teach or preach on this section, it is the checklist for the perfect wife. The problem is that many women are faced with an expectation that they fall short. Men demand that they strive to be like the Pro-Verbs 31 woman. In reality, what the woman needs to do is not strive but to rest in who they are as God molds and shapes the yielded female vessel.

If men would begin to look at their wives through eyes of faith and begin to call things that are not as though they were, they might one day realize that the woman they are married to is an excellent wife.

As I read this list I see many of these qualities in my wife of 43+ years right now. Brenda really is excellent and I have found her. Here is a listing of the proverbial Pro-Verbs 31 Woman (aka The Excellent Wife)

- Her worth is far above jewels
- The heart of her husband trusts in her
- He will have no lack of gain
- She does him good and not evil all the days of her life

- She looks for wool and flax
- She works with her hands in delight
- She is like merchant ships as she brings her food from afar
- She rises also while it is still night and gives food to her household, portions to her maidens
- She considers a field and buys it
- From her earnings she plants a vineyard
- She girds herself with strength
- She makes her arms strong
- She senses that her gain is good
- Her lamp does not go out at night
- She stretches out her hands to the needy
- She is not afraid of the snow for her household
- All her household are clothed with scarlet
- She makes covering for herself
- Her clothing is fine linen and purple
- Her husband is known in the gates when he sits among the elders of the land
- She makes linen garments and sells them
- She supplies belts to the tradesmen
- Strength and dignity are her clothing
- She smiles at the future
- She opens her mouth in wisdom
- The teaching of kindness is on her tongue
- She looks well to the ways of her household
- She does not eat the bread of idleness
- Her children rise up and bless her
- Her husband also, and he praises her

Wow…what a woman! You could spend forever studying Pro-Verbs 31:10-31, but we won't; after all, this is a devotional. Here is what the husband says about the Pro-Verbs 31 woman as he praises her.

"Many daughters have done nobly, but you excel them all. Charm

is deceitful and beauty is vain, but a woman who fears the Lord, she shall be praised, and let her works praise her in the gates."
(Pro-Verbs 31:29-31)

PRAYER: Father, thank You for bringing a Pro-Verbs 31 woman into my life. Lord, I purpose to do what is written in 1 Peter 3:7, which says, *"You husbands likewise, live with your wives in an understanding way, as with a weaker vessel, since she is a woman; and grant her honor as a fellow-heir of the grace of life so that your prayers may not be hindered."* Amen.

DAY 80
THE FIT BATTLE
(You Make Me Wanna SHOUT)

"And the Lord said to Joshua, 'See, I have given Jericho into your hand, with its king and the valiant warriors.'"

(Joshua 6:2)

There is an old spiritual about this battle called, "Joshua Fit The Battle." For years, I never knew what the word *fit* meant, but did enjoy the song, especially the version by Elvis Presley.

I knew from the lyrics that there was a guy named Joshua and there was a battle and that the walls come tumbling down, but again I never could figure out that word *fit*.

Did he have to get in shape before he could enter the battle? Did the walls come tumbling down because he was fit or having a fit?

JOSHUA FIT THE BATTLE OF JERICHO

Joshua fit the battle of Jericho, Jericho, Jericho
Joshua fit the battle of Jericho
The walls come tumblin' down

According to Dictionary.com, the word *fit* has multiple meanings including:

- adapted or suited; appropriate
- proper or becoming
- qualified or competent, as for an office or function
- prepared or ready
- in good physical condition; in good health
- to be adapted to or suitable for (a purpose, object, occasion, etc.)
- to be proper or becoming for
- to be of the right size or shape for
- to adjust or make conform
- to make qualified or competent
- to prepare
- to put with precise placement or adjustment
- to be suitable or proper
- to be of the right size or shape, as a garment for the wearer or any object or part for a thing to which it is applied

Some of these words and definitions may apply to Joshua and the battle but none of them express what Joshua did. I finally found out that the word *fit* meant *fought*. Now, that makes more sense for a battle.

Joshua did fit the battle but realized that he actually fought the battle of Jericho. Whether he fit or fought the battle, the bottom line is that the wall did most definitely come tumbling down.

FOUGHT: lacham (law-kham')=A primitive root; to *feed* on; figuratively to *consume*; by implication to *battle* (as *destruction*): - devour, eat, X ever, fight (-ing), overcome, prevail, (make) war (-ring). (*Strong's*)

JOSHUA FOUGHT THE BATTLE OF JERICHO

> *Joshua fought the battle of Jericho Jericho, Jericho*
> *Joshua fought the battle of Jericho*
> *The walls come tumblin' down*

Joshua fought a battle with a city (actually the people of the city) which was fortified against other human beings. Sometimes the fortification that we use to keep people out is the same fortification that keeps us in. We build walls and towers with our emotions and fears in hope that we do not have to reveal our insecurities.

Randy Matthews was a pioneer of the Jesus Movement, when Jesus was moving through the youth, hippies, and seekers of truth. Randy wrote a song, "It Took a Carpenter," about a carpenter who tore down the walls that he [Randy] had built up over the years. He sang that his own hands were not strong enough to tear down self-made walls. When the Lord looked at him, He made Randy see that he was blind to those walls and needed the Carpenter to tear down his walls.

The city of Jericho was tightly shut because of the sons of Israel. No one was able to go out and no one was able to come in. In the minds of the people within the walls of the city, they were safe and sound. As long as they had their walls, they were protected. They had not factored in the God of Israel. The Lord had already spoken to Joshua about the outcome and the plan to implement so the outcome would become manifested.

> "And the Lord said to Joshua, 'See, I have given Jericho into your hand, with its king and the valiant warriors.'"
> (Joshua 6:2)

God's plan for Joshua and the Israelites is laid out in Joshua 6:3-5.

- You shall march around the city.
- All the men of war circling the city once.
- You shall do so for six days.
- Seven priests shall carry seven trumpets of rams' horns before the Ark of the Covenant.
- On the seventh day, you shall march around the city seven times.

- The priests shall blow the trumpets.
- When they make a long blast with the ram's horn, when you hear the sound of the trumpet, all the people shall *shout* with a *great shout*.
- The wall of the city will fall down flat.
- The people will go up, every man straight ahead.

Joshua the son of Nun gave out the instructions that he had received from the Lord and they assembled together.

NOTE: Some people believed that Joshua was a Catholic since he was the son of a nun. Some believed that he was an orphan since he was the son of none. Sorry, bad joke…but it always puts a smile on my lips.

Now, let us return to the story.

As they gathered to begin the march, Joshua underscored when they were to shout. If I had been involved in that march, I would need a reminder, because the emotions and the anticipation of what was promised might overwhelm me and I would shout prematurely. So, Joshua reiterated when to shout.

> *"But Joshua commanded the people, saying, 'You shall not shout, nor let your voice be heard, nor let a word proceed out of your mouth, until the day I tell you,* shout. *Then you shall* shout!'"
> (Joshua 6:10, emphasis mine)

For full details of the encounter, read Joshua 6:1-27.

There will be another shout, when our Lord returns and gives a *shout*, "Come up hither." Our mortal coil will fall and we will rise to meet Him in the sky to go home.

> *"And they heard a great voice from Heaven saying unto them,*

'Come up hither.' And they ascended up to Heaven in a cloud; and their enemies beheld them."

(Revelation 11:12)

"For the Lord Himself will descend from heaven with a shout, *with the voice of the archangel, and with the trumpet with them in the clouds to meet the Lord in the air, and thus we shall always be with the Lord. Therefore comfort one another with these words."*

(1 Thessalonians 4:16-18, emphasis mine)

PRAYER: Lord, thank You for giving us the ability to not only *shout*, but also the ability to hear Your *shout*. Lord, I am listening, come quickly Lord. Amen.

DAY 81
THE BOOK OF THE TRUE BELIEVERS

"Many other signs therefore Jesus also performed in the presence of the disciples, which are not written in this book; but these have been written that you may believe that Jesus is the Christ, the Son of God; and that believing you may have life in His name."

(John 20:30-31)

I don't recall where I heard this, but I have heard that in the Gospels of Matthew, Mark, Luke, and John are recorded things that Jesus said and did. They cover a thirty-four-year period of time—from the angel's visit to Mary through to His ascension—but when it is distilled down, there might have been three months of actual chronological history on the time-space continuum. I can barely fathom what has been revealed in the Book. I do know that what I have read has positioned me to be a believer with a great hope of life eternal in His name.

BELIEVE: pisteuo (pist-yoo'-o)=From G4102; to *have faith* (in, upon, or with respect to, a person or thing), that is, *credit*; by implication to *entrust* (especially ones spiritual well being to Christ): - believe (-r), commit (to trust), put in trust with. G4102: pistis *(pis'-tis)*=From G3982; *persuasion*, that is, *credence*; moral *conviction* (of *religious* truth, or the truthfulness of God or a religious teacher), especially *reliance* upon Christ for salvation; abstractly *constancy* in such profession; by extension the system of religious (Gospel) *truth* itself: - assurance, belief, believe, faith, fidelity.

G3982: peithō (*pi'-tho*)=A primary verb; to *convince* (by argument, true or false); by analogy to *pacify* or *conciliate* (by other fair means); reflexively or passively to *assent* (to evidence or authority), to *rely* (by inward certainty): - agree, assure, believe, have confidence, be (wax) content, make friend, obey, persuade, trust, yield. (*Strong's*)

Belief is more than just an assimilation of facts that we have rolling around in our minds. Many people believe in many things for many reasons. To be a *true believer*, however, your beliefs must be based on truth. The belief must drop from the mind into the heart and then manifested in actions.

> *"For God so greatly loved and dearly prized the world that He [even] gave up His only begotten (unique) son, so that whoever believes in (trusts in, clings to, relies on) Him shall not perish (come to destruction, be lost) but have eternal (everlasting) life."*
> (John 3:16; The Amplified Bible)

I like the way The Amplified Bible distills the Greek word for *belief* down to the bare essentials.

- Trust in
- Cling/Adheres to
- Relies on

This is more than just mental assent of some facts about something; it is a tenacious relationship with the Son of God.

PRAYER: Lord, I do trust, cling and rely on You for everything in my life. I am a *true believer* in You. Thank You for the revelation of Yourself in what was written in the Book. Amen.

DAY 82
ARE YA BREATHING

"Let everything that has breath, praise the Lord. Praise the Lord!"
(Psalms 150:6)

The Psalms ends with what is entitled, "A Psalm of Praise." During our journey through the Psalms in this devotion have been focused on the goodness of God; His protection; His heartbeat for His people; the laments of the enemy trying to overtake us; and praise that they cannot overtake us because we choose to hide ourselves in Him. They are songs designed to be sung with praise on our lips as the strings are plucked.

Now we are coming to the end of the Psalms in our devotional, and it is another one of those *power psalms* of rowdy praise as we raise some "halal." Once again, I will write the definition of the word, "halal" just to remind you that the "hallelujah" is not limited to quiet times, but to loud times in the Lord.

PRAISE: halal (haw-lal')=A primitive root; to *be clear* (originally of sound, but usually of color); to *shine*; hence to *make a show*; to *boast*; and thus to *be* (clamorously) *foolish*; to *rave*; causatively to *celebrate*; also to *stultify:* - (make) boast (self), celebrate, commend, (deal, make), fool (-ish, -ly), glory, give [light], be (make, feign self) mad (against), give in marriage, [sing, be worthy of] praise, rage, renowned, shine. (*Strong's*)

The title of today's devotion is a *Thanx And A Tip O Da Hat* to my friend, brother, mentor, pastor, and Levite, Wayne Berry. He has been known to say more than once, "Are ya breathing?" As a Speech-Language Pathologist, I am familiar with the process of speaking verbal words. Verbal expression involves breath that is inhaled and then exhaled as words (thoughts) are formed on the lips via the articulators (tongue, soft palate, teeth, alveolar ridge, etc.) as words come out of the mouth on a stream of breath. Are ya breathing?

For praise to come out of your mouths, praise must be on your mind and many times it must be on purpose. Sometimes we may utter, "Praise the Lord," but it may not have distinct meaning. When you focus on the object of the praise, and choose to praise Him on purpose..." run d-evil run." Let's go through Psalm 150, and see to Whom, why, and how this thing called "halal" can be expressed.

- Praise the Lord.
- Praise God in His sanctuary.
- Praise Him in His mighty expanse (firmament).
- Praise Him for His mighty deeds.
- Praise Him according to His excellent greatness.
- Praise Him with trumpet sound.
- Praise Him with harp and lyre.
- Praise Him with timbral and dancing.
- Praise Him with stringed instruments and pipe.
- Praise Him with loud cymbals.
- Praise Him with resounding cymbals.

If you can inhale and exhale, you can choose to *praise the Lord*. If you don't praise the Lord, the rocks will cry out. This is what Jesus told a group of people who were telling the rowdy, "halal-ers" to be quiet.

> *"But Jesus answered, 'I tell you, if these become silent, the stones/ rocks will cry out!'*
>
> (Luke 19:40, addition mine)

Now if a rock that does not have the capacity to breath in and out can cry out…what is stopping us from *praising* (halal) *the Lord?* Are ya breathing?

PRAYER: Lord, forgive me for the times that I stopped the breath flowing with Your praise. *Praise the Lord!*

DAY 83

THE LISTENING CAUSE-AND-EFFECT

"But he who listens to me shall live securely, and shall be at ease from the dread of evil."

(Pro-Verbs 1:33)

LISTEN/HARKEN: shamaʻ (shaw-mah')=A primitive root; to *hear* intelligently (often with implication of attention, obedience, etc.; causatively to *tell*, etc.): - X attentively, call (gather) together, X carefully, X certainly, consent, consider, be content, declare, X diligently, discern, give ear, (cause to, let, make to) hear (-ken, tell), X indeed, listen, make (a) noise, (be) obedient, obey, perceive, (make a) proclaim (-ation), publish, regard, report, shew (forth), (make a) sound, X surely, tell, understand, whosoever [heareth], witness. (*Strong's*)

According to Dictionary.com, the word "hark/harken" means: (1) to listen attentively; hearken (2) to listen to; hear (3) a hunter's shout to hounds, as to encourage them in following the scent. (4) Of hounds to return along the course in order to regain a lost scent (5) to return to a previous subject or point; revert

The book of Pro-Verbs has a thread that weaves itself throughout the entire book. The thread is, if you follow the Lord's wisdom, you will not be foolish and experience the cause-and-effect of your foolishness and disobedience. It is the words of a father to a son. For us, it is the word of the Father to His children.

If you have been reading through this devotional, you may have noticed the way that I spell Proverbs. I spell it Pro-Verbs because it is a book of Pro—or Positive Action—Words—or Verbs; thus Pro (Positive) Verbs (Actions).

It all comes down to the son *listening* to the Father. The word *listen* also means *to harken*. I like the word *harken* because it speaks of listening on purpose and the purpose being to hear what is being said. I especially like the definition from the dictionary in reference to the hound and the hunter, where the hunter shouts words of encouragement to follow the scent and to encourage the dog to return along the course in order to regain a lost scent and to return to a previous point and revert (change directions).

In the world of sheep and shepherds, there is a connection between them with the shepherd's voice. Jesus is the Shepherd and we are His sheep. He speaks, we listen, and avoid danger in a world of wolves.

> *"But you do not believe, because you are not My sheep. My sheep hear My voice, and I know them, and they follow Me; and I give eternal life to them, and they shall never perish; and no one shall snatch them out of My hand. My Father, who has given them to Me, is greater than all; and no one is able to snatch them out of the Father's hand. I and the Father are one."*
>
> (John 10:26-30)

PRAYER: Lord, You are speaking and I am harkening to Your voice. Lord, You have said, "Let Him who has ears to hear…hear." (listen up, perceive) I have ears and I hear You, Lord. Amen.

DAY 84

THE CYCLE OF DELIVERANCE

"And when the sons of Israel cried to the Lord, the Lord raised up a deliverer for the sons of Israel to deliver them..."

(Judges 3:9)

DELIVERER/DELIVER: yasha' (yaw-shah')=A primitive root; properly to *be open, wide* or *free*, that is, (by implication) to *be safe*; causatively to *free* or *succor*: - X at all, avenging, defend, deliver (-er), help, preserve, rescue, be safe, bring (having) salvation, save (-iour), get victory. (*Strong's*)

The children of Israel were chosen and given a promise of freedom. When they were to be released from the slavery of Egypt, God raised up a deliverer long before they cried out for deliverance. God had prepared someone who He would used to set them free.

Throughout their journey towards the Promised Land, they did evil in the sight of the Lord again and again. They would once again cry out for deliverance, and again God's Spirit came on them, judged them, forgave them and delivered them. The would have rest, until they sinned again. Can you say, "a picture of Jesus?"

The judges included in the book of Judges were:

- Otheniel

- Ehud
- Shamgar
- Deborah
- Gideon
- Tola
- Jair
- Jephthah
- Ibzan
- Elon
- Abdon
- Samson

As I read through the book of Judges, I am struck by the faithfulness of God in the face of an unfaithful people. God is faithful in their idolatry; in their immorality and wickedness; and in their cyclical turning away from Him over and over again. As I shake my head and cluck my tongue about the unfaithfulness of Israel and wondering how they could do such a thing, the Lord reminded me…well…of me and the cyclical nature of my sin patterns and the cyclical nature of me coming to Him for forgiveness again. I know that I need to do good, but I don't do it.

> "Therefore, to one who knows the right thing to do, and does not do it, to him it is sin."
>
> (James 4:17)

I join the Apostle Paul in the conundrum of my cyclical sin nature versus being in Christ.

> "For we know that the Law is spiritual; but I am of flesh sold into bondage to sin. For that which I am doing, I do not understand; for I am not practicing what I would like to do, but I am doing the very thing I hate. But if I do the very thing I do not wish to do, I agree with the Law, confessing that it is good. So now, no longer am I the one doing it, but sin which indwells me.

> *For I know that nothing good dwells in me, that is, in my flesh; for the wishing is present in me, but the doing of the good is not. For the good that I wish, I do not do; but I practice the very evil that I do not wish. But if I am doing the very thing I do not wish I am no longer the one doing it, but sin which dwells in me. I find then the principle that evil is present in me, the one who wishes to do good. For I joyfully concur with the law of God in the inner man, but I see a different law in the members of my body, waging war against the law of my mind and making me a prisoner of the law of sin which is in my members. Wretched man that I am! Who will set me free from the body of this death?*
> (Romans 7:14-24)

Paul ends this section with the question, *"Who will set me free from the body of this death?"* The children of Israel cried out for deliverance. The Spirit of God came on human flesh, in the forms of judges and military men who lead them into victory with physical and spiritual rest, until they returned to sin and needed another deliverer.

In answer to Paul's question, God has sent the Ultimate Deliverer where the Spirit of God rested and dwelled and never left Him. There is now no need for multiple deliverers on a human level; our only Deliverer is Christ Jesus. I am reminded of the Texas Ranger motto, "One riot, One Ranger." No need for multiple judges and delivers when you have Jesus the Christ. "One sin nature, one Christ."

The Apostle John points out in his first epistle that even though we are saved, we still sin and need to be released again, and again, and again from the bondage of sin.

> *"And this is the message we have heard from Him and announce to you, that God is light, and in Him there is no darkness at all. If we say that we have fellowship with Him and yet walk in the darkness, we lie and do not practice the truth; but if we walk in*

the light as He Himself is in the light we have fellowship with one another, and the blood of Jesus His Son cleanses us from all sin. If we say that we have no sin, we are deceiving ourselves, and the truth is not in us. If we confess our sins, He is faithful and righteous to forgive us our sins and to cleanse us from all unrighteousness."

(1 John 1:5-9)

PRAYER: Lord, thank You for coming as my Deliverer. I join Paul and say, "Thanks be to God through Jesus Christ our Lord!" Amen!

DAY 85
CHRISTMAS EVE

"And it came about that while they were there the days were completed for her to give birth."

(Luke 2:6)

Well, "Tis the season…" and the big day is tomorrow. I am talking about Christmas Day, the day in which we celebrate the birth of the Savior of the World.

To many, the big day is the unwrapping of presents; the gathering together with friends and families; the climax of all the songs, cards, merriment, the sights, sounds, smells of the season; and all the commercialism of what has come to be known as Christmas.

Now don't get me wrong; I actually love the hoopla and entrapments of what we call Christmas. But I must always, always, get back to the true reason of the season; that being the birth of a baby Who would grow to be the Savior of the world.

Oh, you can poo-poo the baby part and bring out all the facts that no one knows when He was born, and that most likely it could be in April; or you can try to ruin the day for us by pointing out that Christmas is actually an attempt to counter pagan celebration with Christian celebrations. Oooorrrrrr…. you can capitalize on the moment where the focus is on the birth of Jesus and take the opportunity to share your faith.

Historically, it starts with an angel visiting Mary, a young girl who was a virgin and had not has sexual intercourse with a man. Mary was engaged to a man named Joseph. Gabriel rolls in and calls her the *favored one* and tells her *that the Lord is with her.*

This troubled Mary and not just troubled her but it, *"greatly troubled her."*

It troubled her enough to where the Gabe had to calm her down by saying to her, *"Do not be afraid…"* and then underscore again, *"You have found favor with God."* The messenger angel then dropped the new on her:

> *"…you will conceive in your womb, and bear a son, and you shall name Him Jesus. He will be great and will be called the Son of the Most High; and the Lord God will give Him the throne of His father David; and He will reign over the house of Jacob forever; and His kingdom will have no end."*
>
> (Luke 1:31-33)

Mary responded with a logical question:

> *"…how can this be, since I am a virgin?"*
>
> (Luke 1:34)

The angel answered her question with the truth:

> *"The Holy Spirit will come upon you, and the power of the Most High will overshadow you; and for that reason, the holy offspring shall be called the Son of God."*
>
> (Luke 1:35)

The angel then lets Mary know that God has already orchestrated the story with her relative Elizabeth, mother of John who would introduce Jesus into the world. (John 1:36) The angel then underscores the "How can this be?" portion of Mary's question by declaring:

"For nothing will be impossible with God."
(Luke 1:37)

Mary's response is what all eternity is hinged on, as she says to God's messenger who has brought God's Word to her:

"Behold, the bond-slave of the Lord; be it done to me according to your word…"
(Luke 1:38)

As you continue to read the story in the first two chapters of Luke and the first two chapters of Matthew, you see joy, adventure, conspiracy, murder plots, and God's arrangement for prophecy to take place, to get Joseph and Mary where they need to be to give birth at the proper place in the proper time.

After all of these things that took place, Mary and Joseph were together on the eve of the birth of their Son, who would become the King and Savior of the World.

PRAYER: Father, thank You for providing the entrance of the Savior of the world in such an unexpected way in the form of a baby. Amen.

DAY 86
HAPPY BIRTHDAY TO YOU

> *"And she gave birth to her first-born son; and she wrapped Him in cloths and laid Him in a manger, because there was no room for them in the inn."*
>
> (Luke 2:7)

Today, we look at the story in its simplicity, minus the trappings of the world.

The Birth of Jesus (Luke 2:2-20)

> *"In those days Caesar Augustus issued a decree that a census should be taken of the entire Roman world. (This was the first census that took place while Quirinius was governor of Syria.) And everyone went to their own town to register.*
>
> *"So Joseph also went up from the town of Nazareth in Galilee to Judea, to Bethlehem the town of David, because he belonged to the house and line of David. He went there to register with Mary, who was pledged to be married to him and was expecting a child. While they were there, the time came for the baby to be born, and she gave birth to her firstborn, a son. She wrapped Him in cloths and placed Him in a manger, because there was no guest room available for them.*
>
> *"And there were shepherds living out in the fields nearby, keeping watch over their flocks at night. An angel of the Lord appeared*

to them, and the glory of the Lord shone around them, and they were terrified. But the angel said to them, 'Do not be afraid. I bring you good news that will cause great joy for all the people. Today in the town of David a Savior has been born to you; He is the Messiah, the Lord. This will be a sign to you: You will find a baby wrapped in cloths and lying in a manger.'

"*Suddenly a great company of the heavenly host appeared with the angel, praising God and saying,*

"'*Glory to God in the highest heaven, and on earth peace to those on whom His favor rests.*'

"*When the angels had left them and gone into heaven, the shepherds said to one another, 'Let's go to Bethlehem and see this thing that has happened, which the Lord has told us about.'*

"*So, they hurried off and found Mary and Joseph, and the baby, who was lying in the manger. When they had seen Him, they spread the word concerning what had been told them about this child, and all who heard it were amazed at what the shepherds said to them. But Mary treasured up all these things and pondered them in her heart. The shepherds returned, glorifying and praising God for all the things they had heard and seen, which were just as they had been told.*"

Well, that is it. The reason for the season. O, come let us adore Him.

PRAYER: Thank you, Lord. Amen.

DAY 87
THE STRANGE ADULTERESS WOMAN WITH FLATTERING WORDS

"To deliver you from the strange woman, from the adulteress who flatters with her words."

(Pro-Verbs 2:16)

The book of Pro-Verbs gives some good advice out about how to avoid death and destruction. In the book, the temptation many times comes in the form of a woman who entices and tempts. This woman is known as the Strange Adulteress Woman (S.A.W.)

The word *temptation* does not necessarily mean that you have to be pulled into something, albeit that can and does happen. It means to be pulled away from who you are and pulled away from God's purpose for you in your life. Here is a profile on this Strange Adulteress Woman found in Pro-Verbs 2:16-18:

- She flatters with her words (speaks anything to get you to believe a lie)
- She leaves the companion of her youth (if she is unfaithful to her companion, she will be unfaithful to you)
- She forgets the covenant of her God (any agreement that she comes into with you will be just as easily forgotten)
- She has a house that sinks down (bows down) to death (when

you bow down to death you cannot bow down to life at the same time)
- She has tracks that lead to the dead (there is a starting point that ends in death if you choose to track her)

The cause-and-effect of following this Strange Adulteress Woman is that: (1) None who goes to her returns again, (2) None will reach the paths of life. What can you do to avoid the entrapments of the Strange Adulteress Woman?

> *"So you will walk in the way of good men, and keep to the paths of the righteous. For the upright will live (dwell) in the land and the blameless will remain in it."*
> (Pro-Verbs 2:20-21)

> *"But (in contrast to verse 21) the wicked will be cut off from the land, and the treacherous will be uprooted from it."*
> (Pro-Verbs 2:22, addition mine)

I don't know about you, but when you weigh following the S.A.W. (Strange Adulteress Woman) with walking and following way of good men, and keeping to the paths of the righteous versus going with the wicked, and being cut off from the land and being uprooted with the treacherous, that I am going have to go with the good and righteous and say bye-bye to the Strange Adulteress Woman.

Wisdom, who is another lady portrayed throughout the book of Pro-Verbs, is the opposite of the S.A.W. Let's take a look at more of Pro-Verbs 2. Wisdom:

- Does not use her words to manipulate you
- She is faithful and remains with her companion
- She remembers and does not forget her God given covenant/ agreements

- Her house is on a solid foundation of the Rock.
- She takes the Lord at His words when He says, "Follow Me," and she know that His tracks lead to life.

The roots of this Pro-Verb are based in:

- Receiving the Father's sayings
- Treasuring the Father's commandments
- Making your ear to the Father's wisdom (the good woman)
- Inclining your heart to understanding
- Cry out for discernment
- Lift your voice for understanding
- Seek for her (understanding) as silver
- Search for her (understanding) as for hidden treasures

The cause-and-effect for actively seeking the Lord is that you will:

- Discern the fear of the Lord
- Discover the knowledge of God
- Be given wisdom from the Lord
- Have knowledge and understanding coming from His mouth
- Have wisdom stored up for the upright
- He will be a shield to those who walk in integrity
- Your paths of justice will be guarded
- Your ways will be preserved
- You will discern righteousness and justice, equity and every good course
- Wisdom will enter your heart
- Knowledge will be pleasant to your soul
- Discretion will guard you
- Understanding will watch over you

The bottom line is; if you are living like this, you will recognize the Strange Adulteress Woman (S.A.W.) and will avoid her pitfalls.

PRAYER: Lord, thank You for your book of Positive Action (Pro-Verbs) that reveals to me how to live and walk by faith and not by sight. Amen.

DAY 88
THAT'S THE POWER OF LOVE

"Many waters cannot quench love, nor will rivers overflow it; if a man were to give all the riches of his house for love, it would be utterly despised."

(Song of Songs 8:7)

LOVE: 'ahabah (a-hab-aw')=Feminine of H158 and meaning the same: - love. **H158: 'ahab** *(ah'-hab)*=From H157; *affection* (in a good or a bad sense): - love (-r). **H157: 'ahab 'aheb** (aw-hab', aw-habe')=A primitive root; to *have affection* for (sexually or otherwise): - (be-) love (-d, -ly, -r), like, friend. (*Strong's*)

This book is a song of love and marriage between a man and a woman, between a king and a Jewish maiden. Various commentaries break down the song in three parts: (1) courtship (2) the preparation for a wedding (3) the marriage. This natural process of emotion between a man and woman gives a beautiful picture been the bride and the bridegroom, between the Christ and the Church. The world would pervert the pure love and attempt to make it dirty.

Love is the expression that God has for the world and the motivator for sending His Son to planet Earth to become a tangible manifestation of that love. In the Greek language, there are four aspects of this crazy little thing called love. In English, we may have one word to express many aspects of love, while in the Greek we have many words that express the characteristics of love. For Solomon and his maiden, the *eros* love is palpable in his sensual song.

- *Eros* is the sensual love.
- *Phileo* is the brotherly love between mankind.
- *Storge'* is a familial love between family.
- *Agape* is the love of God that is pure.

Each of these loves in their self is a good thing, but when each one becomes defiled by selfishness, it turns into lust which turns into sin which results in death.

> *"Each one is tempted when he is carried away and enticed by his own lust. Then when lust has conceived, it gives birth to sin; and when sin is accomplished, it brings forth death."*
> (James 1:14-15)

When true love is in bloom between a man and a woman, it cannot be quenched or overflowed.

QUENCHED: kabah (kaw-baw')=A primitive root; to *expire* or (causatively) to *extinguish* (fire, light, anger): - go (put) out, quench. (*Strong's*)

OVERFLOW: shataph (shaw-taf')=A primitive root; to *gush*; by implication to *inundate*, *cleanse*; by analogy to *gallop*, *conquer*: - drown, (over-)flow (-whelm), rinse, run, rush, (throughly) wash (away). (*Strong's*)

> *"For God so loved the world that He gave His only begotten Son, that whosoever would believe (trust in, cling to, rely upon, adhere to) in Him should not perish (be quenched or overflowed) but have everlasting life."*
> (John 3:16, addition mine)

PRAYER: Lord, You loved me first and I respond back by loving You.

Nothing will quench or overflow the love You have for me and mine for You. Amen.

DAY 89
LIVING BREAD: GLUTEN FREE

"I am the bread of life."

(John 6:48)

There is an old saying; "Bread is the staff of life."

STAFF: matteh mattâh (mat-teh', mat-taw')= a *branch* (as *extending*); figuratively a *tribe*; also a *rod*, whether for chastising (figuratively *correction*), ruling (a *sceptre*), throwing (a *lance*), or walking (a *staff*; figuratively a *support* of life, for example bread): - rod, staff, tribe. (*Strong's*)

> *"When I break your* staff of bread *ten women will bake your bread in one oven, and they will bring back your bread in rationed amounts, so that you will eat and not be satisfied."*
> (Leviticus 26:26, emphasis mine)

It appears that this idea of the "staff of life" is what is used for support. Whatever "staff of life" means, Jesus is our staff, our support for living.

Jesus' statement that He is the Bread of Life is preceded by an event that Jesus was using to test Philip about how they were going to feed all those people who were coming.

> *"Jesus therefore lifting up His eyes, and seeing that a great multitude was coming to Him, said to Philip, 'Where are we to buy*

> *bread that these may eat?' And this He was saying to test him; for He Himself knew what He was intending to do."*
>
> (John 6:5-6)

This was when there were around 5,000 people listening to Jesus teach and they were fed with five barely loaves and two fish. The food was distributed and everyone had as much as they wanted and they were filled. At the end, there was enough to fill twelve baskets with fragments which were left over by those who had eaten. (John 6:1-13)

The people again were looking for a sign but Jesus recognized their motives and confronted them.

> *"Jesus answered them and said, 'Truly, truly, I say to you, "You seek Me, not because you saw signs, but because you ate of the loaves, and were filled. Do not work for the food which perishes, but for the food which endures to eternal life, which the Son of Man shall give you, for on Him the Father, even God has set His seal."'*
>
> (John 6:26-27)

Once again, Jesus is taking a natural event, like food and eating, and turning it into a lesson Him. The people referenced their past about how their fathers ate the manna (supernatural provision) in the wilderness.

Jesus turns it back on them and points out that it was His Father who gave them manna and not Moses. Jesus speaks of *"true bread"* that came down of Heaven and that He is the *"True Bread"* who has come out of Heaven for them.

> *"Jesus therefore said to them, 'Truly, truly, I say to you, it is* not Moses who has given you the bread out of heaven *(manna), but it is My Father who gives you the* true bread *out of heaven. For*

> *the* bread of God *is that which comes down out of heaven and gives life to the world.*'"
>
> (John 6:32-33, addition and emphasis mine)

When the people heard this, they wanted that bread. Remember, that these were the same people who had eaten miracle bread.

> *"He said therefore to them, 'I am the bread of life; he who comes to Me shall not hunger, and he who believes in Me shall never thirst.'"*
>
> (John 6:35)

Everyone who had seen had not believed and even began to grumble against Him. It appears that the thing that would keep them fed and not thirsty was the same thing that would trip them up.

> *"The Jews therefore were grumbling about Him, because He said, 'I am the bread that came down out of heaven.'"*
>
> (John 6:41)

How often Jesus tells us point-blank who He is and point-blank how we can access Him by faith, by trusting in, clinging to, and relying upon His words. The bottom line, according to Jesus, in John 6:36-40:

- You have seen Me and yet do not believe.
- All that the Father gives Me shall come to Me.
- The one who comes to Me I will not cast out.
- I have come down from Heaven not to do My own will but to do the will of Him who sent Me.
- This is the will of Him who sent Me, that of all that He has given Me, I lose nothing, but raise it up on the last day.
- This is the will of My Father, that everyone who beholds the Son, believes in Him, may have eternal life and I Myself will raise him up on the last day.

They were blinded by the truth because of their unbelief. Just like grumbling kept their fathers out of the Promised Land, so their grumbling will keep them from dining on the Bread of Life.

This is where we came in. Jesus declared once again Who He was:

> *"I am the Bread of Life. Your fathers ate the manna in the wilderness, and they died. This is the bread which comes down out of heaven, so that one may eat of it and not die. I am the Living Bread that came down out of heaven; if anyone eats of this bread, he shall live forever; and the bread also which I shall give for the life of the world is My flesh."*
>
> (John 6:48-51)

Now they had something else to grumble and argue about trying to make it out like Jesus was talking about cannibalism by equating the bread to His flesh and drinking His blood.

PRAYER: Forgive me for grumbling and complaining and arguing with others about Who You are. Thank You for the bread of Your body and the drink of Your blood and that I never have to hunger and thirst again. Amen.

DAY 90
REVIVE ME AGAIN, AND AGAIN, AND AGAIN

"My soul cleaves to the dust; revive me according to Thy Word."
(Psalm 119:25)

I love those old western movies where the weary cowboy has been out in the dust storms and they walk into the local bar parched with their tongue cleaves to the roof of their mouth, and they walk up to the bar, slap down their money and say, "Whiskey!"

Well, the weary traveler in the world has the same problem; only it is their soul that cleaves to the dust and they need reviving. So, the weary traveler, the sojourner strolls into the bar, slaps down the money and cries out, "Thy Word!"

As we close out this book with the Psalms, I thought I would glean from the longest Psalm, Psalm 119. There are 176 verses in this Psalm, and they all point to the Word of God in some form or fashion. The Psalm written as an acrostic (a series of lines or verses in which the first, last, or other particular letters when taken in order spell out a word, phrase) poem, where the 176 verses are divided into 22 stanzas with each stanza starting with a name based on a letter of the Hebrew alphabet. Each stanza praises the Word of God.

Today, I will glean out of each stanza something about the Word of God.

- Aleph: *Oh, that my ways may be established to keep Thy statues* (119:5)
- Beth: *How can a young man keep his way pure? By keeping it according to Thy Word.* (Psalm 119:9)
- Gimel: *Deal bountifully with Thy servant that I may live and keep Thy Word.* (119:17)
- Daleth: *My soul cleaves to the dust; revive me according to Thy Word.* (119:25)
- He: *Make me walk in the path of Thy commandments, for I delight in it.* (119:35)
- Vav: *And I will walk at liberty* (a wide place), *for I seek Thy precepts.* (119:45)
- Zayin: *The arrogant utterly deride me, yet I do not turn aside from Thy Law.* (119:51)
- Heth: *The Lord is my portion; I have promised to keep Thy Word.* (119:57)
- Teth: *The law of Thy mouth is better to me than thousands of gold and silver pieces.* (119:72)
- Yodh: *May Thy compassion come to me that I may live, for Thy Law is my delight.* (119:77)
- Kaph: *My soul languishes for Thy salvation; I wait for Thy Word.* (119:81)
- Lamedh: *Forever, O Lord, Thy word is settled in heaven.* (119:89)
- Mem: *O how I love Thy law! It is my meditation all day long.* (119:97)
- Nun: *Thy word is a lamp to my feet, and a light to my path.* (119:105)
- Samekh: *Thou are my hiding place and my shield; I wait for Thy Word.* (119:114)
- Ayin: *Therefore, I love Thy commandments above gold, yes above fine gold.* (119:127)
- Pe: *I opened my mouth wide and panted, for I longed for Thy commandments.* (119:131)
- Tsadhe: *Thy word is very pure, therefore Thy servant loves it.* (119:140)
- Ooph: *I rise before dawn and cry for help; I wait for Thy words.* (119:147)

- Resh: *Consider how I love Thy precepts; revive me, O Lord, according to Thy lovingkindness.* (119:159)
- Shin: *Seven times a day I praise Thee, because of Thy righteous ordinances.* (119:164)
- Tav: *Let my tongue sing of Thy Word.* (119:172)

His Word is a magnificent thing. It is not only wonderfully written and preserved on the pages of the Bible, it is alive and written on our hearts.

> "For the Word that God speaks is alive and full of power [making it active, operative, energizing, and effective]; it is sharper than any two-edged sword, penetrating to the dividing line of the breath of life (soul) and the [immortal] spirit, and of joints and marrow [of the deepest parts of our nature], exposing and sifting and analyzing and judging the very thoughts and purposes of the heart."
> (Hebrews 4:12/The Amplified Bible)

No wonder the psalmist wrote such a long psalm about the Word of God. The thoughts, intents, and heartbeat of God are written within in each word.

PRAYER: Lord, thank You for speaking and singing to me via Your Word in the Psalms. Lord, I love to sing along with You in Your active and living songbook. Amen.

DAY 91
FOUNDED AND ESTABLISHED

"The Lord by wisdom founded the earth; by understanding He established the heavens."

(Pro-Verbs 3:19)

"In the beginning God created the heavens and the earth."

(Genesis 1:1)

In the book of Genesis (the book of beginnings), we see God going through the motions of the physical act of creation by speaking it into existence. But we need to realize that this creation was not a whim but a grand design. God had a thought (what He was speaking), then God spoke a word (what He was thing thinking), and then God had an action (creation). But God did all of this with wisdom and understanding.

WISDOM: chokmâh (khok-maw')=From H2449; *wisdom* (in a good sense): - skillful, wisdom, wisely, wit. **H2449: châkam (**khaw-kam')=A primitive root, to *be wise* (in mind, word or act): - X exceeding, teach wisdom, be (make self, shew self) wise, deal (never so) wisely, make wiser. (*Strong's*)

FOUNDED: yâsad (yaw-sad')=A primitive root; to *set* (literally or figuratively); intensively to *found*; reflexively to *sit* down together, that is, *settle, consult:* - appoint, take counsel, establish, (lay the, lay for a) found (-ation), instruct, lay, ordain, set, X sure. (*Strong's*)

UNDERSTANDING: tâbûn tebûnâh tôbûnâh (taw-boon', teb-oo-naw', to-boo-naw')=*intelligence*; by implication an *argument*; by extension *caprice:* - discretion, reason, skilfulness, understanding, wisdom. (*Strong's*)

ESTABLISHED: kûn (koon)=A primitive root; properly to *be erect* (that is, stand perpendicular);. hence (causatively) to *set up*, in a great variety of applications, whether literal (*establish, fix, prepare, apply*), or figurative (*appoint, render sure, proper* or *prosperous*): - certain (-ty), confirm, direct, faithfulness, fashion, fasten, firm, be fitted, be fixed, frame, be meet, ordain, order, perfect, (make) preparation, prepare (self), provide, make provision, (be, make) ready, right, set (aright, fast, forth), be stable, (e-) stablish, stand, tarry, X very deed. (*Strong's*)

We see that the earth was not founded on foolishness and that the heavens were not established by some misunderstanding. No, there was skillful and discretion in the creation of the world. Prior to the creation, the world was in a chaotic state without form, void, and dark. The Holy Spirit was hovering and sweeping over this chaos like a mother hen brooding over her chicks in anticipation of the cracking of the egg and the revelation of the creation. God spoke a word over the chaos and brought order to dis-order.

A word of wisdom and a word of understanding were spoken by God in the form of The Word.

> *"In the beginning was the Word and the Word was with God and the Word was God. He was in the beginning with God. All things came into being through Him; and apart from Him nothing came into being that has come into being. In Him was life; and the life was the light of men. And the light shines in the darkness; and the darkness did not comprehend it."*
> (John 1:1-4)

> *"There was a true light which, coming into the world enlightens*

> *every man. He was in the world, and the world was made through Him, and the world did not know Him. He came to His own, and those who were His own did not receive Him. But as many as received Him, to them He gave the right to become children of God, even to those who believe in His name, who were born not of blood, nor of the will of the flesh, nor of the will of man, but of God. And the Word became flesh and dwelt among us, and we beheld His glory, glory as of the only begotten from the Father, full of grace and truth."*
>
> (John 1:9-14)

Who is this Word? His name is Jesus. If you go back and insert the name "Jesus," where ever you see the word, "word," it will become evident that this man Jesus was closely involved with wisdom and understanding in the foundation and establishment of the world.

The writer of Hebrews also points to Jesus as the Creator of the world.

> *"God, after He spoke long ago to the fathers in the prophets in many portions and in many ways, in these last days has spoken to us in His Son (Jesus), whom He appointed heir of all things, through whom also He made the world. And He is the radiance of His glory and the exact representation of His nature, and upholds all things by the word of His power. When He had made purification of sins, He sat down at the right hand of the majesty on high; having become as much better than the angels, as He has inherited a more excellent name than they."*
>
> (Hebrews 1:1-4)

PRAYER: Lord, I thank You that You gave me a sure foundation and have established me for purpose. I thank You that I am a new creation in Christ and the old things have passed away and behold new things are constantly coming in my life. Amen.

DAY 92

FALLEN (WOUNDED) RISEN (HEALED)

> *"All of us like sheep have gone astray, each of us has turned to his own way; but the Lord has caused the iniquity of us all to fall on Him."*
>
> (Isaiah 53:6)

When Adam and Eve choose to disobey God, their sin caused them to fall from the grace of God. The cause-and-effect was sin passed down to us.

> *"Therefore, just as through one man (Adam) sin entered into the world (the fallen state) and death by sin (cause-and-effect), and so death spread to all men, because all sinned—"*
>
> (Romans 5:12, addition mine)

Isaiah prophecies of another falling, but this time it will be sin that falls. This sin, this iniquity, falls off of us and onto Him so that we will not be bound with death. The suffering Messiah suffers in our place as the propitiation (satisfactory substitute) for our iniquity. Like sheep we had gone astray, away from the shepherd. We have turned to our own way that seems right but the end is destruction.

> *"There is a way which seems right to a man, but its end is the way of death."*
>
> (Pro-Verbs 14:12)

In the Amplified Bible, Isaiah 53:4-5 speaks of how we are healed.

- Surely, He (Jesus) has borne our griefs (sickness, weakness and distress)
- And carried our sorrows and pain of punishment
- Yet we ignorantly considered Him stricken, smitten and afflicted by God as if with leprosy
- But (in contrast)
- He was wounded for our transgressions
- He was bruised for our guilt and iniquities
- The chastisement needful to obtain the well-being for us was upon Him
- With/By His stripes that wounded Him we are healed and made whole

Some theologians state that this merely describes how God dealt with sins (things as a result of the sin nature). Others see that, not only did He deal with the nature of sin, but also the cause-and-effect of sin which includes physical healing.

In the book of Matthew, we see Isaiah 53:4 in reference to physical healings. A leper had been healed (Matthew 8:1-4); a centurion's (Roman soldier) servant was healed (Matthew 8:5-13); and then Jesus went into Peter's home and saw Peter's mother-in-law sick in bed with a fever. Jesus touched her hand and the fever left her and she arose and began to wait on Him. (Matthew 8:14-15).

People began to bring to Jesus people who were demon-possessed and He cast out the spirits with a word, and He also *healed all* who were ill.

At this point, Matthew points out that these physical healings were evidence that what Isaiah had spoken was fulfilled. Now, this does not mean that there was no need for further healing, since Isaiah 53:4 was fulfilled as evidence by Jesus continuing on with more healings. It simply underscored that Jesus was not only the Savior for sins, but also for physical healing.

> *"Surely He has borne our griefs—sickness, weakness and distress—and carried our sorrows and pain [of punishment]. Yet we ignorantly considered Him stricken, smitten and afflicted by God [as if with leprosy]. But He was wounded for our transgressions, He was bruised for our guilt and iniquities; the chastisement needful to obtain peace and well-being for us was upon Him, and with the stripes that wounded Him we are healed and made whole."*
>
> (Isaiah 53:4-5; The Amplified Bible)

HEALED: rapha' raphah (raw-faw', raw-faw') = A primitive root; properly to *mend* (by stitching), that is, (figuratively) to *cure*: - cure, (cause to) heal, physician, repair, X thoroughly, make whole. **H7503: raphah (raw-faw')** = A primitive root; to *slacken* (in many applications, literally or figuratively): - abate, cease, consume, draw [toward evening], fail, (be) faint, be (wax) feeble, forsake, idle, leave, let alone (go, down), (be) slack, stay, be still, be slothful, (be) weak (-en). (*Strong's*)

PRAYER: Lord, thank You for everything You did for me on the cross. I thank You that I am forgiven for my sin and iniquity, and also You are the Healer for my sickness and disease. Lord, when I went my own way like a sheep gone astray, You found me and allowed me to be free from sin. Amen.

CLOSING THOUGHTS

We have come to an end not only of *Chewing the Daily Cud, Volume 4*, but also the final book in the four-volume set of *Chewing the Daily Cud*.

It has been an honor to chew the cud of the Word of God with you. My prayer is that you were drawn closer to the Lord by drawing closer to His Word and that your life will be affected for the better.

Also Available From:
WordCrafts Press

Trusting God in Testing Times
   by Jill Grossman

Confounding the Wise
   by Dan Kulp

Pondering(s)
   by Wayne Berry

Ditch the Drama
   by Ginny Priz

Morning Mist; *Stories from the Water's Edge*
   by Barbie Loflin

Youth Ministry is Easy!
   and 9 other lies
   by Aaron Shaver

I Am
   by Summer McKinney

Pressing Forward
   April Poynter

www.wordcrafts.net

CPSIA information can be obtained
at www.ICGtesting.com
Printed in the USA
LVHW030756231121
704193LV00003B/29

9 780999 647547